Our Times

Our Times

The *Washington Times* 1982–2002

Edited by

Lee Edwards

Since 1947
REGNERY
PUBLISHING, INC.
An Eagle Publishing Company • Washington, DC

Library of Congress Cataloging-in-Publication Data
Our Times : the Washington times, 1982-2002 / edited by Lee Edwards.
    p. cm.
Includes index.
ISBN 0-89526-178-2

1. Washington times (Washington, D.C. : 1982) I. Edwards, Lee.
PN4899.W285 O95 2002
071'.53—dc21

                                                          2002002362

Published in the United States by

Regnery Publishing, Inc.
An Eagle Publishing Company
One Massachusetts Avenue, NW
Washington, DC 20001

Visit us at www.regnery.com

Distributed to the trade by

National Book Network
4720-A Boston Way
Lanham, MD 20706

Printed on acid-free paper
Manufactured in the United States of America

10 9 8 7 6 5 4 3 2 1

Books are available in quantity for promotional or premium use. Write to
Director of Special Sales, Regnery Publishing, Inc., One Massachusetts
Avenue, NW, Washington, DC 20001, for information on discounts and
terms or call (202) 216-0600.

Contents

Foreword

I am delighted that Washington has a strong voice that is unafraid to present the conservative viewpoint in its editorials and whose news coverage is far more balanced than its competitors.

We are a proud and patriotic country. The *Washington Times* understands that and *Our Times* reflects that as well.

I was very proud to be president at a time of dramatic change in the world. *Our Times* gives the reader a scholarly insight into much of that change in the world. *Our Times* also talks about basic American values and honors them.

Today our country is united and strong. The *Washington Times* has been very supportive of our president, which, I am sure, is appreciated in the White House and across our country. It is surely appreciated by his proud father.

Read this collection of essays, and whether or not you agree with every point in every essay, you will feel better about our future.

Respectfully submitted,

George Bush
41st President USA

Introduction

From an era in which few believed the Berlin Wall would ever fall, to one in which the world was forced to believe the Twin Towers could fall; from the March for Life's celebration of humanity, to the slow drip of Dr. Death's suicide machine; from the sunny smile of Ronald Reagan, to the diabolic visage of Osama bin Laden, *Our Times* is a dual history. It looks at the extraordinary events of the last twenty years and at the unique role of a new daily newspaper—the *Washington Times*—in reporting and often helping to make history during this revolutionary era. *Our Times* is the collective effort of several of the most distinguished historians and authors in the nation, and indeed the world, to examine what happened and why.

In the lead essay, British historian Paul Johnson provides a sweeping overview, beginning with the triumvirate that appeared at almost the same time—Pope John Paul II, British prime minister Margaret Thatcher, and President Ronald Reagan. He recounts how their inherently complementary policies created a powerful tide for global freedom and democracy. Johnson ends by examining the two challenges of terrorism and globalism and says, "The *Washington Times*, during its first twenty years, has never had any doubt about America's duty to carry [her] burdens and her will and capacity to discharge them with honor."

Drawing from my experiences as an editor and professor of politics, my own essay focuses on the revolutionary changes in the mass media over the last twenty years—such as the birth of CNN, the explosive growth of talk radio, and the phenomenon of the Internet—and how these new media have changed the way that Americans practice their politics. I argue that in today's media environment, when many journalists are careless about the power they wield, the need for a traditional gatekeeper such as the *Washington Times*, especially in Washington, D.C., is greater than ever before.

Harvard professor and Russia scholar Richard Pipes examines the last decade of the Cold War and burrows into the cause of the December 1991 disintegration of the Soviet Union. His dissection of Soviet history reveals that the communist state was doomed to collapse from the start because its founding principles were hopelessly contradictory and utopian. Pipes says that a major external cause of the Soviet breakup was the containment policy initiated by President Harry Truman. It was continued by every successive president until Ronald Reagan and George H. W. Bush went on the offensive and targeted the Soviet Union, politically, economically, and strategically, at every opportunity.

Social critic and author Midge Decter describes the Culture War since 1992—an era replete with battles over abortion, welfare reform, gay rights, and affirmative action. Although her analysis is somber in tone, Decter concludes on a hopeful note, writing that the resurgence of patriotism and the celebration of American family values in the wake of September 11 augers well for the future. She notes the *Washington Times*'s significant contribution to the Culture War through its profamily position on issues such as partial-birth abortion, "gangsta" rap recordings, and public education.

In the concluding essay, columnist and Hoover Institution research fellow Arnold Beichman describes the deep pessimism of many in the West in the early 1980s and how an always optimistic President Reagan revived a moribund economy and brought down an evil empire through military strength and resolute diplomacy. He draws a parallel between the radical New Left of a quarter century ago and a twenty-first-century New Left marked, in the words of public intellectual Richard Posner, by intellectual arrogance and a proclivity for taking extreme positions. Beichman writes that the *Washington Times* has become one of the nation's leading newspapers because its reporters and editors enjoy broad editorial freedom and have used the freedom to make an exemplary contribution to the battle of ideas. Confirmation of the *Washington Times*'s indispensable role in the nation's capital was provided by President George W. Bush, who told the newspaper's editor in chief, "You're a conscience of this town."

Our Times captures a remarkable era of American history and shows how a new daily newspaper has become—in just twenty years—a national symbol of independence and dependability as it has realized the vision of its founder, the Reverend Sun Myung Moon, to counter totalitarianism and immorality through the telling of unfashionable truths. It has been a privilege to work with people such as Paul Johnson, Richard Pipes, Midge Decter, and Arnold Beichman who take their history seriously, and to help produce a work which we hope will be used by teachers and students who want to study two of the most important decades in American history. I wish to thank all the editors, reporters, librarians, and other employees of the *Times* who gave so generously of their time and attention, especially Douglas D. M. Joo, the president of the *Washington Times*.

—LEE EDWARDS

The
Globalization
of American
Values

PAUL JOHNSON

Paul Johnson

Paul Johnson, a British journalist and historian based in London, is the author of dozens of books. *A History of the American People*, *Modern Times*, and *Intellectuals* are among his most widely known and influential.

he first twenty years of the *Washington Times*'s existence form one of the most interesting and unpredictable periods in the history of humankind, and a supremely difficult test for a new daily newspaper. Centuries do not close or open epochs, much as methodical historians would like them to. The twentieth century closed with the implosion of the Soviet Empire in 1989. The twenty-first opened with the explosion of large-scale global terrorism on September 11, 2001. The intervening period was one of confusion and uncertainty, in which geostrategists struggled to find a new pattern of stresses which had replaced the Cold War. What in fact was happening, as we can now discern clearly, was that the world was converging to form a unified plane of action, and the war against terrorism, declared by President George W. Bush immediately after the events of September 11, 2001, was the first episode in the new unified globe.

Globalization, hitherto seen as a commercial and economic phenomenon, now appeared as a political, military, and diplomatic one, too. Tony Blair, the British prime minister, called it "the war for civilization against the forces of violence, barbarism, and chaos." In more than one sense it was: it marked the point at which civilization, as defined by the West—a culture over two thousand years old, based on Greco-Roman and Judeo-Christian patterns of behavior, enriched by capitalism, the Industrial Revolution, and the continuing Information Age—was finally asserted to be the necessary pattern for the entire planet.

This marked a huge change in historical and geographical perspective. The Greeks had divided the known world into the *oikumene* of Greek culture, marked by all the civilized institutions of the polis (odeon, gymnasium, academy, stadium, etc.) and the darkness outside it, which they called, quite literally, chaos. The Romans had the Empire, and beyond it, barbarism. In the Middle Ages there was Christendom, Byzantium, Islam, and the pagan east. The nineteenth century saw emerging a Europeanized world of colonies and former colonies, which itself was destroyed by Europe's two civil wars. When the second ended, a new order emerged, first baptized by the French writer Maurice Duverger in *Le Monde*: The "first world" of the West, liberal and democratic; the "second world" of communism, totalitarian and collectivist; and the "third world" of the poor states with vast and rising populations, low incomes, and despairing aspirations. The Cold War, which lasted the best part of half a century, offered a kind of stability. Since 1949, NATO had defined trip wire frontiers, across which the Soviets must not trespass without risking global thermonuclear war. Equally, the "Brezhnev Doctrine" laid down that once a state had become part of the Soviet bloc, the West could attempt to "liberate" it only at its peril. The geopolitical struggle, therefore, was essentially waged only in the Third World, as West and East struggled for its allegiance, giving aid, arms, and "advisers."

The Soviet Union never came close to winning the Cold War as such. In the context of "competitive coexistence," Khrushchev's famous threat, "We will bury you," proved vacuous, for the Soviet economy was outperformed by the West by any standard of measurement. However, in the 1970s, the Soviet Union appeared to be making spectacular progress in the Third World.

During a power vacuum in Washington, marked by the aborted presidency of Richard Nixon, the unelected presidency of Gerald Ford, and the weak single term of Jimmy Carter, Congress virtually seized control of foreign and military policy, imposing unprecedented restrictions on the freedom of the executive to protect U.S. interests. During this time, Russia, using its surrogates, Cuba and Vietnam, was able to Sovietize a number of territories in Asia and Africa, and operate powerfully and at will in vast regions hitherto dominated by the U.S. and her allies. It became a commonplace among left-leaning academics to proclaim the Soviet advance as irresistible and the American "empire" as past its apogee and in inevitable decline.

But history is made primarily by the willpower of great human personalities rather than by anonymous forces. At the end of the 1970s, three events changed its course. The first was the election of Pope John Paul II in October 1978, the second the parliamentary victory of Margaret Thatcher in Britain in May 1979, and the third the election of Ronald Reagan as U.S. president in November 1980. Between them, these three remarkable leaders turned the world around. The new pope, a fervent Polish nationalist, directed a spiritual dagger at the heart of Soviet power in Poland, the largest and weakest link in the communist empire. The alliance between a militant Catholic Church and Polish free trade unionism proved unbeatable, and Poland began the accelerating process whereby the Soviet Empire disintegrated.

Margaret Thatcher's victory might not have proved significant, for Britain was only a medium-sized power, but for her astonishing determination to reject compromise in the fervent pursuit of her libertarian beliefs and the manner in which she captured the imagination of millions at home and abroad. Not only did she break the power of Britain's left-wing unions, by forcing them into two major pitched battles and beating them off the field, she began the process of reducing Britain's inefficient and ruinously costly public sector by what she called "privatization": selling off nationalized industries to the people in public flotations. This process proved so popular that it was soon copied in more than fifty countries.

Mrs. Thatcher also made it plain that, in defense and foreign policy, the drift of the 1970s would be halted and reversed. Britain, of course, was not in a position to do this alone. But it became apparent in the course of 1980 that she had a notable admirer and follower in the Republican candidate, and once Mr.

Reagan was elected, he began not merely to reestablish the constitutional force of the executive vis-à-vis the legislature, but to use this restored power with massive authority, and in a Thatcherite direction. But, of course, Reagan was his own man, with a few simple, central, sensible, and popular ideas about running the government—and astonishingly skillful gifts in communicating them. He was not a replica of Mrs. Thatcher, but the two complemented each other and quickly established a cloudless working partnership.

Mr. Reagan had nothing to privatize. But he deregulated the economy and reduced taxes. He ignored warnings about the yawning federal budget deficit, believing that his measures to reenergize the economy would in time double tax revenue. Indeed, he joked about it: "I'm not too worried about the deficit," he told a press conference. "It's big enough to take care of itself." So it proved, adding substance to the illuminating maxim that Reagan "governed by jokes." He set the economy on course for the biggest and longest boom in its history, so that well before the end of the century the budget was in surplus and debt was being systematically repaid.

Hence by 1982, the year the *Washington Times* was launched, the trio who were to destroy the Soviet Union were well established in power, and the process was under way. The new paper gave warm and systematic support to all three. It also extended a particular welcome to the almost visionary policy which came to form perhaps the most significant element in the new Reagan geopolitics. This was the Strategic Defense Initiative, popularly known as Star Wars. Reagan believed America was becoming dangerously underarmed, and he quickly took measures to redress this weakness over the whole military spectrum. He also believed that the "balance of terror" used to maintain the Cold War peace was fundamentally immoral, unstable, benefited the Soviets, and had indeed in the 1970s led to the expansion of what he now baptized "the evil empire."

Persuaded it was now possible to create an antimissile shield, which would eventually be able to destroy all incoming Soviet missiles, and had the added advantage of protecting America from rogue states which had somehow acquired nuclear weapons—a growing threat throughout this period—Reagan gave the project his support, and it went ahead.

The SDI had an uncovenanted result: it demoralized Soviet geopolitical planners, who eventually grasped that their country had neither the technology nor the resources to match the American effort. The realization brought to a head a growing crisis of self-confidence among the Soviet elite, centered on the current performance of the command economy, and future projections. There were also five specific factors which undermined the regime. The first was the costly failure to conquer Afghanistan, part of the forward-pushing adventurism which marked Soviet policy in the 1970s. The adventure began in 1978; by the next year eighty thousand Soviet troops were in the country, and the figure soon rose to 120,000. The fighting lasted a decade during which sixteen thousand Soviet troops were killed and thirty thousand wounded, a million Afghans died and six million, a third of the population, became refugees. By 1988 Moscow gave up in despair, and Soviet troops, having accomplished nothing, were withdrawn by February 1989.

The Soviet debacle in Afghanistan was hastened, if not caused, by the policy known as the Reagan Doctrine, under which the U.S. government supported insurgents against communist power in Afghanistan, Nicaragua, and Angola. The *Washington Times* offered strong support for that policy, support the president acknowledged at the paper's tenth anniversary when he said in a video address, "Together we won the Cold War."

The second factor was a series of demoralizing accidents demonstrating the fragility of Soviet technology. In April 1986 the nuclear reactor at Chernobyl, near Kiev, blew up—the worst calamity of the entire nuclear era. In August, a large Soviet passenger liner sank in the Black Sea with the loss of four hundred lives. In October a Soviet nuclear submarine, with sixteen hydrogen bomb warheads, sank without trace or apparent cause, mid-Atlantic. An earthquake killed twenty thousand people, making the relief services look impotent. A gas leak from a Soviet pipeline blew up two crowded passenger trains, killing eight hundred people. Ominous long-term factors of stagnation and decline made themselves felt. The birthrate in Greater Russia, the demographic core of the Soviet Union, declined to less than 1 percent, against 2.5 to 3.6 percent for Soviet Muslims, among whom knowledge of the Russian language was declining and who were becoming less "Russian," let alone Sovietized. The total "demographic deficit" caused by wars, famines, massacres, and purges during the Soviet period was sixty million. By the beginning of the 1980s, there were 137 million Great Russians—an aging population—against fifty million Muslims, whose average age was much lower.

Demographic problems were compounded by the growing inability of the regime to feed its people. The agricultural decline reached back to the earliest years of communism, compounded by the collectivization policy, the slaughter of Kulaks or "rich peasants" (i.e., the most efficient), and the drift of farm workers to the towns. Decline became precipitous after the disastrous harvest of 1963, which prompted Khrushchev to ask: "Why should meat and eggs be unobtainable [in Russia] after fifty years of Soviet power?" He added: "I look forward to the day when a camel would be able to walk from Moscow to Vladivostok without being eaten by hungry peasants on the way." Though the Soviet Union had twice as much land under cultivation as any other country on earth, including soil of superlative quality in the Ukraine, its need to import food, especially cereals, rose, reaching fifteen million tons of cereals in some years and as much as thirty million in others. During the last days of the regime and after, attempts at "reform" made matters worse. It was calculated that, lacking a proper market system, 40 percent of the food produced never reached the consumers: it simply rotted in warehouses and railway sidings. By the winter of 1990–91 there was a real threat of starvation in Russia. Rationing was reintroduced and the authorities were forced to beg for Western food aid. Rationing by price was introduced too, but that hit the poorest. During the referendum held on March 16, 1991, to determine whether the Soviet Union should remain a unity, the authorities tried to encourage a high turnout of its supporters by selling food, from its secret stores, at polling stations—but even that had run out by midday. At the bottom of all the regime's difficulties was a theory based on dishonest use of statistical evidence—Marx's forte—compounded by sheer ignorance. No Marxist ever seems to have held sensible views on growing food. Neither Marx nor Lenin was interested in it: Marxism-Leninism was essentially an urban religion. Yet the Soviet performance in industry was not essentially better, though concealed by fake figures. When fairly accurate statistics began to be available in the 1990s, it was realized that the actual GNP of Russia was not essentially higher than the Netherlands.

After the long rule of Brezhnev, later termed "the period of stagnation," leaders came and went. First, in 1982, there was Yuri Andropov. He lasted seven months, dying in office. His successor, Konstantin Chernenko, lived for only a year before dying in his turn. Then, in 1985, came a youngish man, Mikhail Gorbachev, a liberal communist, who accepted that the regime was in a mess but believed it could be reformed within the assumptions of Marxism. This fundamental fallacy was reflected in his opening declaration, the first part of which was contradicted by the second: "We have to change everything; I am a Communist." He thus began the impossible task of trying to improve a system which was beyond redemption and could only be scrapped.

But in one respect Gorbachev did introduce radical change. He decided that in the light of the Afghanistan disaster, the Soviet Union could no longer be held together by force. He made it clear to the leaders of the Soviet satellites in Europe that they were on their own: they must introduce reforms quickly to quiet popular discontent or face the public's wrath without Soviet aid. The Red Army, which had intervened in Hungary in 1956 and Czechoslovakia in 1968, would stay in its barracks. Hungary took the first step, introducing "market factors" into its "command economy." But reform came too late to save communism.

Poland, which had been a major food exporter in the 1930s, experienced an agricultural disaster almost on the scale of Russia's, and this, combined with the growing popular power of the Catholic Church and the free trade-union movement, led to the ousting of the communist regime headed by Wojciech Jaruzelski. On June 5, 1989, it suffered a crushing defeat in free elections demanded by popular protest movements. In September, the first noncommunist government took over in Warsaw.

The failure of the Kremlin to rescue its satraps by force led to the collapse of all its dominoes in Europe. In October, the Communist Party of Hungary voted itself out of existence. In November, communism collapsed in East Germany, and the Berlin Wall was pulled down. The same month Czechoslovakia put in a popular government under Vaclav Havel, and in December the communist regime in Bulgaria was replaced. On December 21, TV viewers in the West saw live the strange spectacle of Nicolae Ceausescu, the brutal dictator of Rumania,

booed and abused by a hostile crowd when he appeared on the balcony of his palace. After a series of riots, listeners all over the world heard over the radio the sound of Christmas bells on December 25, a moving message that Rumania, too, was now a free country.

Communism did not immediately collapse all over the world. In March 1989, riots by Tibetans against the Chinese occupation were put down savagely. In April student riots broke out in Beijing, and the demonstrators occupied Tiananmen Square in the heart of the city. On May 30, they erected in the square a thirty-foot fiber and glass replica of the Statue of Liberty. This goaded the hesitant authorities into action. Using huge numbers of infantry and columns of tanks, the regime cleared the square, killing 2,400 students and wounding ten thousand. Similar military action took place in other major Chinese cities, and the country continued to be ruled by communists. However, these rulers also embarked on a systematic liberalization of the economy, introducing elements of the market system and novel versions of capitalism. These produced results in terms of supplies of food and consumer goods, raising living standards and incomes, and so took some of the heat out of the demand for political change.

China was able, by agreement, to absorb the highly successful Hong Kong economy, where the one hundred-year-old British lease had run out, and Hong Kong methods were widely imitated in Shanghai and other Chinese commercial cities. By the turn of the century, China, though still a communist dictatorship, was a semi-market economy, with one of the world's highest growth rates: an anomaly, since freedom is indivisible in the long term, which would clearly be resolved at some point by the introduction of democracy.

By contrast, in Russia, neither the "evil empire" nor communism itself proved durable. Gorbachev himself, who had barely survived a determined conspiracy by old Stalinist hard-liners and the secret police, was eventually ousted by the genial figure of Boris Yeltsin, who became the first Russian president to be elected directly (June 1991), securing over 60 percent of the popular vote. Yeltsin was a regionalist rather than a centralist like Gorbachev, and it was natural for him to preside over a dissolution of the USSR, whose constituent parts, from the Baltic States occupied by Stalin in 1940, to the southern and Asian components of the old tsarist empire, chose to go their separate ways. With them went Communist Party domination in most cases, though party apparatchiks everywhere, including in Russia itself, showed a protean ability to survive under different labels. The government of Yeltsin, who was reelected and then, in time, handed over peacefully to his successor, Vladimir Putin, was essentially post-communist, trying with very limited success to introduce an efficient market system. By the opening years of the twenty-first century, Russia was still the second largest military power but by any economic yardstick was a shattered hulk, whose recovery, begun under Putin, would take decades.

The leaders of the West looked on with astonishment rather than pure delight at this sudden transformation of the once powerful enemy. State Departments and Foreign Offices tend to prefer to deal with large accumulations of power and territory rather than ungovernable multitudes of petty states. "Balkanization" is a term of abuse in their vocabulary. Ronald Reagan would no doubt have applauded the dismantlement of the Soviet Empire, and the eclipse of Russian communism. But he had gracefully exited early in 1989 after one of the most successful presidencies, at home and abroad, in American history. The harvest of his geopolitical sowing was reaped by his vice president and successor, George Bush, who took a more conventional view of power. He did his limited best to keep the old Soviet Union together and went so far as to appeal to the Ukrainians not to choose independence—no doubt because the Ukraine inherited, as a separate state, a portion of the USSR's nuclear arsenal, and America preferred to negotiate with one nuclear power rather than two.

America, helped by Britain and France, also tried to keep Yugoslavia, the major communist power in the Balkans, from disintegration in the wake of the collapse of the USSR. It had originally been created by Britain and France in 1918 precisely to prevent "Balkanization." But the regime was unpopular both because it was communist and because it was Serb. It also, being Orthodox, had religious differences both with the Catholic Slovenes, Croatians and Dalmatians, and with the Muslim Bosnians.

The West wanted unity in Russia and Yugoslavia because it feared the alternative was war. It was proved wrong in Russia, but right in the Balkans. The Serbs were obliged to let Slovenia go. But they would allow Croatia independence only at the price of a large portion of Croatian territory. Moreover, they proceeded to make their occupation permanent by a policy of what they called "ethnic cleansing"—in fact, amounting to the wholesale murder of the non-Serb population.

This was a form of genocide and provoked worldwide protest and Western intervention. In the case of Croatia, arms purchases in the West allowed the new state to establish its freedom by force, and to reconquer some of its lost land. But when the Yugoslav army began to apply the same technique to Bosnia (and, later, Kosovo), the West (in the shape of NATO) was forced to go much further, and eventually to deploy large numbers of American, British, and French troops. A full-scale conflict with Serbia was averted, and eventually the Serbs themselves overthrew the hard-line Communist/Nationalist regime, and even cooperated, to a limited extent, in handing over generals and politicians identified as "war criminals" for trial in the Hague Court.

This horrific series of episodes, which lasted for most of the 1990s, devastated large areas of the country and left a legacy of bitterness which threatened at any time to erupt into fresh violence. It also raised the whole question of how the world was to be policed, now that the Cold War was over and the risk of a thermonuclear catastrophe had receded. After the unpunished aggressions of the 1970s, Reagan and Thatcher had introduced a different response to violation of frontiers. In 1982 the Argentines had conducted an unprovoked and unannounced invasion of the British colony of the Falkland Islands. Thatcher took the view that any such aggression, anywhere in the world, must be punished and reversed, or the planet would slowly dissolve into anarchy and rule by the strong. Receiving sympathy, but no effective assistance from the UN, she assembled an expeditionary force to reconquer the islands, and declared a large area of the South Atlantic a zone prohibited to warships. The force achieved both its local object, of liberating the Falklands, and its wider one, of punishing aggression. Indeed it went further, for in the wake of humiliating defeat, the military junta in Buenos Aires was overthrown, so Thatcher did ordinary Argentines a favor, too. Britain's hazardous campaign, eight thousand miles from home, was assisted by covert U.S. provision of intelligence, and this was significant: it marked a rebirth of the "special relationship" between America and Britain, especially in military and intelligence cooperation, which was soon to produce results all over the world.

The end of the Cold War produced another effect: it made the UN a more effective forum for discussing threats to peace and taking steps to resolve them. Automatic vetoes by Russia (and even China) in the Security Council were no longer routine, and it became possible to persuade the Security Council and the General Assembly to debate rationally and act sensibly when peace was in jeopardy, instead of dividing on Cold War lines. But, in practice, the UN had no divisions, and while it could encourage and approve, the actual provision of measures to deter or reverse aggression was left to the West, under Anglo-American leadership. This new order in world affairs was put sensationally to the test on August 2, 1990, when, without warning, Iraqi forces invaded and occupied Kuwait, richest of the small Gulf oil-states, in the course of a single day. By a fortunate chance, this brutal act coincided with a meeting at Aspen, Colorado, attended by both President George Bush and Margaret Thatcher. Within twenty-four hours they had devised and begun to implement a joint Anglo-American approach which remained unaltered and purposeful throughout the many tense months of diplomacy and military buildup which followed, and during the actual conflict. Bush and Thatcher determined from the start not merely to protect Saudi Arabia (Saddam Hussein's next target) by force, but to liberate Kuwait, whatever it cost, as Thatcher had liberated the Falklands, thus reversing the aggression and punishing the aggressors by armed force. They also agreed to proceed at every stage with the full backing of the UN and to build up the most broadly based international force possible, including Arab states. Before the end of August, a series of Security Council resolutions declared the tragic occupation of Kuwait unlawful, null and void, imposed sanctions, and authorized the use of force to make sanctions work. "All necessary means" were to be used to expel Iraqi forces if they had not left by a deadline of January 15, 1991.

Before the deadline expired America and Britain had organized and deployed a force recruited from twenty-eight different nations, including most Arab ones. Russia did not participate, but approved of the Allied strategy in detail following a Bush-Gorbachev summit in Paris on November 19. Immediately after the UN ultimatum ran out, an Allied air offensive, involving 140,000 sorties, began, followed by a land assault on February 24. This was so successful that by February 28, forty out of forty-two Iraqi divisions had been knocked out or surrendered, and Bush, alarmed by the huge scale of Iraqi losses— fifty thousand killed and 175,000 missing or captured, against Allied losses of 166 dead, 207 wounded, and 106 missing— ordered a cease-fire, allowing Saddam to accept the settlement laid down by the Allies. By this time, Thatcher had resigned as British prime minister, being succeeded by the colorless and unspirited John Major. If Thatcher had still been at Bush's elbow, she would have insisted that the Allied force proceed to Baghdad, overthrow Saddam's dictatorship, and hold free elections under UN control.

But Bush felt constrained to fulfill the UN mandate to the letter, which unfortunately surrendered much of the fruits of his stunning victory. Saddam was left in power and, despite many U.S. and British interventions by force, continued to evade his international obligations and try to manufacture weapons of mass destruction. All the same, Operation Desert Storm achieved lasting results, introducing an era in which America, the world's sole superpower, could act as an international policeman with the backing of the UN, the active support of its chief allies, and the tacit agreement of what had once been the Communist world. The campaign also had a salutary effect on American morale, erasing memories of Vietnam and underlining the power of the West to reverse aggression and so deter it.

In the aftermath of the disappearance of the Soviet Union, the collapse of communism as a working ideology, and the emergence of capitalist America as a sole superpower, some excited conclusions were drawn. The 1990s were seen as "the end of history," in which ideological competition ceased and liberal market capitalism emerged as the only basis on which a nation and its economy could be organized. It is true that a large portion of the world turned to Western models to enrich themselves, with varying degrees of success. But it was clear that it was not enough to press the buttons marked "Capitalism" or

"Market Economy" and expect miracles to occur. The relative failure of Russia to make the market work well for her, despite huge quantities of American financial aid (or perhaps because of it), compared with the success of China in liberalizing its economy and stimulating self-sustaining growth, pointed to the importance of cultural and racial characteristics, notably the existence of an entrepreneurial, competitive, and commercial spirit, in making the new freedom work.

Then there was the case of the European Union which, while steadily enlarging itself to take in states of central, northern, and Eastern Europe, showed a distinct reluctance, under French ideological leadership, to embrace the liberal American model of market capitalism. While proceeding towards a common currency, the Euro, which became a fact for most members in January 2002, as the first step towards the creation of a unified superstate, the EU insisted on innumerable restrictions on entrepreneurial freedom and a leading role for its dirigiste bureaucracy in Brussels. If it was capitalism, it was certainly state capitalism, moving towards the largest controlling authority—the future superstate—in the history of mankind. Here, it seemed, was a halfway house between the United States and the old Soviet command economy.

A second alternative was provided by the Far East—not only by China's market communism, but by the kind of capitalism which had emerged in Japan. This was controlled and directed behind the scenes by a complex, almost mystic, combination of bureaucrats, politicians, bankers, and entrepreneurs. It enjoyed for a time phenomenal success. Beginning in 1953, Japan embarked on a quarter century of growth averaging about 9.7 percent a year. Between the end of the 1950s and the 1970s, Japanese car production increased one hundred times, reaching over ten million in 1979, the American total, and soon passing it. Japan ousted America as the leading producer of radios in the 1960s, of TV sets in the 1970s, and of many other commodities. By 1980 her investment was twice America's per capita, and in some years during the 1980s exceeded it in absolute terms. This spectacular performance of Japan, contrasted with Europe's and America's, was attributed to many things, chiefly education.

By 1990, 93 percent of Japan's children attended secondary schools to the age of eighteen, and about 35 percent went on to tertiary education at the country's one thousand-plus universities and colleges. Other Far Eastern or Southeast Asian states—the "Asian Tigers"—prospered and educated themselves to high standards, especially in the new computer technologies: South Korea, Hong Kong, Taiwan, and Singapore formed a top tier, with living standards approximating Western ones by the end of the 1980s, and Malaysia, Thailand, the Philippines, and Indonesia forming a second tier of states apparently emerging from Third World to First World status.

But during the latter part of the 1980s, and still more in the 1990s, doubts were cast on the reliability of the Asian model of capitalism by the failure to maintain the rapid advances of the past quarter century, and by outright recession. It was not so much recession itself, which was to be expected in capitalist

economies periodically, as evidence of more deep-rooted weaknesses. During the 1990s the currencies of all these states fell in
relation to the U.S. dollar, and the effects in the second tier were
very serious, leading to political instability and abrupt changes
of government. The fall against the dollar reflected a reduction
in, and in some cases a flight of, investment capital, and the
political unrest accelerated the process.

At the same time, evidence emerged, especially in Japan, of
an entirely new phenomenon: overinvestment, creating surplus
capacity for which there were no markets, despite success in
keeping out Western goods and in maintaining huge export sur-
pluses. Moreover, this overinvestment in industry had occurred
at the expense of the banks, which by the late 1980s had accumulated huge debts and were in effect insolvent though kept in
being by state manipulation. Hence Japan entered a long period
of stagnation, which continued into the twenty-first century.
The Japanese miracle was over, though nobody quite knew why.
However, the failure of Japan to maintain its pace in high technology innovation, and the recapture by the U.S. of its leadership in this field, which became a decisive economic fact during
the 1990s, suggested a clue. By successfully keeping out imports,
Japan had kept out ideas too, and by maintaining an economy
directed behind the scenes by industrial-government-banking
cartels, it had also diminished internal competition including
the competition of ideas. Thus the "miracle," having exhausted
the Western ideas it had capitalized on, ran out of cerebral
steam, and ceased to function. The regime, being unwilling to

allow major bankruptcies and unemployment, merely prolonged the stagnation. There was, in short, something fundamental lacking in the Japanese system: freedom. It was not a true market economy, and that is why the Japanese version of capitalism began to look inadequate before the century was out.

A comparable, though different, malaise began to infect continental Europe during the 1990s. Unemployment rose everywhere, but particularly in France, Spain, Germany, and Italy, often reaching and surpassing the 10 percent mark. Germany ceased to be the reliable draught engine of Europe. Inflation remained low in most EU states, but so did productivity gains and growth rates. It was evident that the paternalism or dirigisme provided kept the states out of catastrophic trouble, but could no more provide consistent growth than the cartel manipulation practiced in Japan. By contrast, the British economy, which, thanks to the Thatcher reforms, more closely resembled the American model than the continental European one, grew faster in the 1990s than any other EU state. As a result, Britain's GNP, which had slipped behind France's, then Italy's, moved up to occupy the fourth place in the world league, after the U.S., Japan, and Germany. It continued to perform better than any other European state when recession finally hit the world in 2001.

Meanwhile, the United States, theoretically and in practice the freest of the major economies, enjoyed two decades of unprecedented expansion and prosperity, fueled indeed by a particular boom in high-tech communications products and processes, but more generally by an all-around performance of the economy which was almost a perfect model of how capitalism should function. Inflation remained low or even negative in some years. Virtually full employment was maintained throughout the decade. Productivity rose. While taxes were reduced (along with regulation), the revenue rose as a result of growth—thus proving the basic premise of the once despised "Reaganomics"—the budget went into surplus, and debt was reduced accordingly. If the trade balance remained in deficit, this was offset by America's continuing reputation as the world's best country in which to invest, and by the remarkable strength of the dollar against virtually all other currencies, making it the favored trading currency.

Much of this could be attributed to the efforts of the Reagan administration—and the Bush one which followed it—to promote economic freedom, which led to the founding of a million new businesses, half of them by women, and the creation of thirty million new jobs. But in 1992, after three Republican presidential terms, during much of which the Republicans controlled the Senate, the Democrats regained control of the White House. John Maynard Keynes had often attributed the success of capitalism to "high animal spirits" on the part of entrepreneurs. The new president, William Jefferson Clinton, certainly possessed them to an exceptional degree, plus a political charm which made him a first-class campaigner and easy winner in two elections. But his animal spirits were directed not so much to wealth creation as to other forms of creativity. He arrived in the

White House with a long record of misbehavior and illegalities from his days as governor of Arkansas. And he promptly began to add to them. The *Washington Times* began to cast a suspicious eye on Clinton even before his inauguration, and it gradually devoted more attention to his peccadilloes, and worse, than did any other major American newspaper. Public interest centered on his sexual adventures, and later on his perjured attempts, under oath, to deny the truth.

The *Washington Times* gave these extensive coverage, but it also, alone at first, reported his cryptic relations with Communist China, the gist of which was that the Beijing government made funds available for Clinton's election campaigns in return

for the administration bending or ignoring the rules over dealings with China. When, in response to growing public concern over Clinton's disreputable behavior, a special prosecutor was appointed and Congress embarked upon impeachment, it is unfortunate that the case did not concentrate upon the China aspect—by far the most serious. Instead, Clinton's sex life and lying became the center of the prosecution's case to the virtual exclusion of almost everything else. The result was predictable: Clinton was shamed, the nation was disgusted (as much by the prosecution as by the defense), but the requisite senatorial majority to remove the president from office was never in sight. Clinton served his time out and continued to enjoy some measure of popular approval until his eleventh hour pardons list, amnestying criminals to whom he and his wife were indebted, finally outraged even his most faithful supporters.

Clinton's misdeeds and impeachment had an uncovenanted consequence, brilliantly illustrating Karl Popper's Law of Unintended Effect. Clinton was a born interferer in nature's economic laws, and his strong-minded wife even more so. After a dozen years of Reagan-Bush freedom and deregulation, Clinton's fingers itched to manipulate the economy and create new institutions, following the manner of Franklin Delano Roosevelt and Lyndon B. Johnson, in health, welfare, and public enterprise. In practice, barring a largely abortive scheme for expanding public health care, he did virtually nothing. Almost from first to last his administration was occupied in fending off criticism of his behavior. Clinton's mind and energies were largely, and at times exclusively, devoted to defending himself. As a result the economy, throughout his eight-year presidency, was left alone. Thus favored, it continued to flourish mightily, demonstrating once again that a market capitalist economy, left to regulate itself, tends to produce excellent results. Of course Clinton himself benefited from this benign economic climate, and his ratings remained high. He took the credit for results which his enforced inactivity made possible. Thus unwittingly, Clinton's sexual antics kept America's economy healthier than at any time in its history.

Unfortunately, Clinton's preoccupations also made him inattentive in foreign and defense policy. It was fortunate indeed that the virtual collapse of Russia as a great power and the end of the Cold War introduced a period of comparatively low tension. Clinton never had to deal with a first-rate crisis. But long-term precautions were neglected. The Iraq War of 1990–91 had seen Saddam use his medium-range Scud missiles against Israel. In response, President Bush had sent to Israel Patriot antimissile batteries, which performed well in the circumstances. This reanimated the whole question of an antimissile defensive system, which Ronald Reagan had first brought into the arena of practical politics. Bush continued the work Reagan had begun, but during Clinton's eight years in office the project was pushed into the background and languished.

This was unfortunate, more particularly because the object of an antimissile screen had been enlarged, since the end of the contest with Russia, to include protection against rogue states or terrorist organizations which might, in the foreseeable future, get their hands on nuclear weapons and delivery systems. Modern, organized terrorism, using the communist device of the cell system, was historically an Israeli invention, a product of their struggle against British rule in the decade 1939–48: the Irgun, of which the future Israeli prime minister Menachem Begin was a former leader, being the prototype. But such methods were soon turned against the Israeli state by dispossessed Palestinian Arabs, and organized Arab terrorism became a feature of Middle Eastern life from the 1950s onwards. There were many terrorist groups in the world by the closing decade of the century, often cooperating with each other.

One of the difficulties in dealing with them was that governments, including Western ones, distinguished between different terrorists. The American government, for instance, tolerated the existence of Noraid, a body which collected money in the U.S. to fund the IRA terrorists who operated in British territory—not only in Ulster but in England, where increasingly large-scale explosions, costing many lives, were a feature of the 1980s and 1990s. France allowed a variety of terrorist groups to have offices in Paris, including the notorious Persian Mullah Khomeini, and even helped him to return to Iran, where his supporters overthrew the shah's government, set up a Muslim fundamentalist regime, and became a haven for Islamic terrorist groups in turn. London, too, housed a large number of Arab organizations, some of which had terrorist links. From the end of the 1970s the serious study of international terrorism revealed the size and nature of this growing problem. An Israeli officer, Jonathan Netanyahu, was killed in a successful raid at Entebbe, where Arab terrorists were holding a group of Israelis prisoner. As a result, his brother Benjamin (later Israeli prime minister), set up an organization, the Jonathan Institute, specifically to study international terrorism and to persuade Western states to take measures against it.

At its second conference in Washington in 1984,* the U.S. secretary of state, George Schultz, was persuaded to speak and made a vigorous condemnation of such activities as a threat to international order, the first sign that America was prepared to take the threat seriously. Indeed it had increasingly compelling reasons to do so. On October 23, 1983, two coordinated suicide bomb attacks in Beirut killed 241 American marines and fifty-eight French paratroopers, guarding their embassies. On April 13, 1986, Middle Eastern terrorists blew up a West Berlin discotheque frequented by U.S. troops, and on April 5, 1988, they destroyed in the air a Pan-Am 747 over Lockerbie in Scotland, killing all 258 passengers and crew and eleven on the ground.

The precise responsibility for these attacks remained in doubt. But on July 8, 1985, Ronald Reagan named five nations, Iran, North Korea, Cuba, Nicaragua, and Libya, as "members of

---

* I made the keynote speech on this occasion, printed in London in *The Times*, August 10, 1984, under the headline "Wanted: World War on Terror." This adumbrated virtually all the arguments used by George W. Bush seventeen years later, and the steps he proposed to take to pursue the war.

a confederation of terrorist states," which were carrying out "outright acts of war" against the United States. They were "outlaw states run by the strangest collection of misfits, loony-tunes, and squalid criminals since the advent of the Third Reich." He privately regarded Colonel Gadaffi of Libya as the most dangerous, arguing that "he's not only a barbarian, he's flaky." After the Berlin disco bomb, U.S. intercepts established beyond doubt that Libya was involved, and on April 13, 1986, Reagan authorized an air attack by U.S. F-111 bombers on Gadaffi's military headquarters and barracks in Tripoli. Margaret Thatcher readily gave permission for the F-111s to operate from their NATO bases in Britain, but it was significant that both France and Italy, despite their own problems with terrorism, refused to allow the aircraft to fly over their territory, necessitating a one thousand-mile detour. The notions of collective security against international terrorism had not yet taken root.

It required American willpower and resources to make it practicable. However, at the time both Reagan and his successor, George Bush, had other priorities and preoccupations: how to deal with a disintegrating Soviet Union and its consequences. As it happened, they also believed that the decline of Soviet power, and still more its will to make life difficult for the West, would end in a sharp reduction of Soviet aid for terrorists (and military assistance to states harboring terrorist organizations) and aid supplied by other communist states such as Cuba and North Korea. This hope proved justified in the sense that, during the 1990s, communist aid to terrorism largely ceased—Czechoslovakia, for instance, cut off supplies of high-intensity explosives (semtex) to the IRA immediately after a free government was formed in Prague, though it ruefully admitted that it had already handed over "enough to last them a hundred years." Russia, indeed, rapidly discovered that it had as much to fear from terrorist attacks as any Western state. The disintegration of the USSR reignited its two hundred-year problem of dealing with the Chechens, who remained inside the new and smaller Russia but who wanted their own independent state. Russia's bloody, costly, and for the time being, successful, suppression of Chechen insurgents led to thousands of their "freedom fighters" fleeing to set up terrorist networks or, since they were Muslims, joining existing ones in the Middle East. From there, and from within Russia, they organized bomb attacks in Moscow and other centers of population, killing hundreds of ordinary Russians.

The problem of international terrorism, indeed, was changing its nature. The "Communist Factor" disappeared from the equation. It was replaced, in a violently enlarged form, by the "Muslim Fundamentalist Factor." The "Arab Factor" had always been there, of course, since the emergence of the Palestinian problem in its modern form in 1948. That remained unsolved, and a focus of international tension, Arab bitterness, and sporadic violence half-a-century later. But a feature of the second half of the twentieth century was the emergence of religious fanaticism in virtually all states with a Muslim majority. This was a reversal of a historic trend towards secularism which had begun in Turkey in the 1920s, under Ataturk. It took the form of

Muslim extremists seizing power, as in Iran, and later in Pakistan, Afghanistan, and half-a-dozen other states, and imposing a religious system of law, drawn directly from the Koran and in all essentials going back not merely to medieval times but to the Dark Ages of the seventh and eighth centuries, in its social and moral assumptions. It was particularly severe on women, who were accorded no rights and treated as the mere property of their menfolk. But it also revived the concept of the Holy War, and focused it on the Israeli-Palestinian dispute. This was seen as an invasion and occupation of Islamic territory (rather like the Christian crusades) by one infidel race (the Jews), backed and financed by another, the Americans. Together they represented the "cosmopolitan" forces of modernism in its most repellent and ungodly form, which it was the duty and mission of militant Islam to exterminate.

There was a large element of Jew-hatred in this campaign. As far back as the 1920s, the Mufti of Jerusalem had made anti-Jewish feeling the hallmark of Arab nationalism in Palestine, and he later formed an alliance with Hitler and the Nazis to expel the British. *Mein Kampf* continued to be sold in Arab bookshops until the end of the century and beyond, alongside the notorious anti-Semitic tract, *The Protocols of the Elders of Zion*. In Syria, for instance, schoolchildren were taught that it was God's will that the faithful should destroy all Jews, not only in Israel but in the United States too. Some of the characteristics of Nazi Germany, therefore, reemerged in the Arab Middle East. Elsewhere the focus was on American godless modernism as the source of all wickedness. Khomeini identified America as "the Great Satan," the Muslim equivalent of the Antichrist, a slogan taken up with varying numbers of decibels throughout the Muslim world. Attacks on U.S. property, and the killing of Americans, became a virtuous act, and suicide bombers were told by their mullahs that they would go straight to heaven.

During the eight years of the Clinton presidency, this new threat, or rather the new, intensified version of the old one, was disregarded. That was not for want of provocation, and accumulating evidence of growing power, capacity, and professionalism on the part of the terrorist networks, especially one run by a Saudi millionaire, Osama bin Laden, first from the Sudan, then from the fundamentalist protection of the Taliban regime in Afghanistan. On three occasions during his presidency, Clinton, following terrorist incidents, made strident threats of retaliation, swearing that the U.S. would make war on the networks and the states which harbored them—at various times, no fewer than twelve Muslim states were mentioned. But these verbal offenses were followed only by minor and ineffective military action. The concept of the "War on Terrorism," though often spoken about, did not take shape. Clinton had other things to do.

His successor, George W. Bush, was involved in a close and disputed election, which got his presidency off to a shaky start. However, among his first decisions was to press ahead with a missile defense system with all deliberate speed, on the assumption that nuclear weapons and delivery systems would continue to proliferate, and that, sooner or later, one or more such weapons would fall into the hands of a rogue state or organization determined to use them regardless of the consequences. All the same, the threat was treated as long-term rather than imminent. The events of September 11, 2001, came as a complete surprise, though premonitions had not been lacking: indeed, the New York World Trade Center had been the target of a bin Laden attack during Clinton's presidency, and had provoked one of his verbal counterblasts. Nevertheless, it did surprise the administration, though not to the same extent as the *Washington Times*, which had repeatedly warned about the growing audacity of terrorists and the failure of the United States to take measures against them. Since the days of Watergate, in the mid-1970s, U.S. intelligence agencies had been unappreciated, underfunded, restricted by legal and congressional prohibitions, and had found it difficult to catch the ear of the White House.

All that changed in the days following September 11. Restrictions on CIA activities were lifted, long-term plans set on foot to expedite the creation of antiterrorist forces on land, sea, and air, and, more directly, the decision was taken, in conjunction with Britain and other friendly states, to mount a direct assault on bin Laden's refuge, Afghanistan, unless its regime surrendered the man (and his associates) now identified (and confirmed by his own public admission) as the director of the assault which cost between three to four thousand American lives. As in the case of the Kuwait invasion, an international coalition was formed, with UN authorization, to mount what George W. Bush called "the war for civilization." Again, over a score of states made direct contributions, and more than fifty were involved in one way or another. As an illustration of the way the world had moved on since the end of the Cold War, on this occasion, China, which had its own growing problem with Muslim militants among its minority peoples, gave clearance to America's war plans. Russia not only approved, but cooperated directly in securing landing rights for U.S. forces at airfields in neighboring states, and even provided special service troops. Indeed, as the capitalist-communist polarization receded into history, the concept of a global coalition of law-abiding, civilized states began to take concrete and visible form. Such cooperation, as in the nineteenth-century combination of the Great Powers to put down slavery and piracy, and to intervene in lawless states— as in the suppression of the Boxer Rebellion in China—had been ended by that source of all modern disasters, the First World War, followed so quickly by the Second, and the long confrontation with Russia that emerged from it.

Now at last, at the opening of the twenty-first century, all the sources of legitimate, or at any rate stable, power in the world were coming together to defend the international order against insurgents who, whatever their religious pretensions, appeared to recognize no practical moral code at all. As a result of this unprecedented alignment of major nations, American and British forces, later assisted by others, were able to begin the air assault on the bin Laden-Taliban forces as early as mid-November, and the land operations a fortnight later. They continue successfully at the time of this writing.

International cooperation against terrorism was yet another aspect of a phenomenon which was increasingly a topic of conversation and concern at the beginning of the twenty-first century: globalization. The world was moving together and many found this frightening. They saw it as essentially a feature of capitalism, blamed the United States as its prime mover, and to it attributed many threats to humanity, real or imaginary, such as "global warming." Whether the world was getting warmer, as it had done on numerous occasions in history, and if so whether the process was due to human activity such as the emission of deleterious gasses, remained a matter of scientific argument. One of George W. Bush's early decisions, on becoming president, was to refuse to implement the so-called Kyoto Accords, agreed to by his predecessor, which would have imposed catastrophic restrictions on U.S. business, and on the economy as a whole, just at a time when it was finally, after unprecedented growth, moving into recession anyway. Bush's decision, unpopular among the chattering classes in the West, and denounced in the Third World, which was exempt from punishment under the accords, was not made lightly. The U.S. had, in fact, devoted more money and scientific man-hours to the study of global warming than the rest of the world put together, and a consensus of such research was a nonproven verdict. In that circumstance, Bush was justified in declining to permit self-inflicted wounds on the American economy.

As for globalization itself, identified with many evils such as the destruction of village life, deforestation, ecological damage, and cultural conformism, it had all the characteristics of a natural phenomenon, which had been going on at least as long as the human race itself. Homo sapien, in origin African, according to the latest research, had globalized himself, over a million years. All culture had local origins, and when it proved itself useful, as with farming, the invention of the wheel, and the smelting of iron, spread over the globe. Indeed, globalization is undoubtedly prehuman, since all living things, from plants to mammals, tend to spread if they are fit enough to survive, and there are no natural limits to their colonization of territory. Darwin's work is a commentary on the globalization of species. It might be said, in fact, that the whole of history is the story of globalization, to be followed in due course by the story of universalization, as human beings learn to colonize planets and stars, a process already begun by space travel.

It is right to see America as the prime mover of globalization today, at the beginning of the twenty-first century. But it has many predecessors, notably Greece, whose concept of the *oikumene* was an early globalization project; Rome; China; Venice; Spain and Portugal; the Netherlands; France; Britain; and all states that have created empires expressive of approved and popular norms. America is merely following a well-trodden path, opened up not least by the spread of education and the diffusion of the English language, a demotic globalizing force independent of any government or system, which spreads by convenience—not policy. English or broken English is now spoken in some form by perhaps three billion people: the most widely used expressions on earth are "OK" and "Coca-Cola." The anglicizing of language has been, of course, immensely accelerated by the explosion of new communication technology which was the chief economic feature of the last quarter of the twentieth century. In a growing number of professions, knowledge of, and communication in, English is a prerequisite. But who would argue that the emergence of a global language is a setback for mankind? Does it not finally reverse that global calamity symbolized in the Bible by the Tower of Babel? The fact that soldiers from many lands use English to communicate in Afghanistan while suppressing terrorism is another illustration of the way in which globalization assists civilization to preserve and extend itself.

Hence history seems to suggest that America, committed by its size, success and wealth to take the lead in globalization, has no need to feel ashamed of its role. It entered the twenty-first century burdened by heavy responsibilities, and has added to them since. The *Washington Times* during its first twenty years has never had any doubt about America's duty to carry such burdens and about her will and capacity to discharge them with honor. That is a record to be proud of.

The
Millennium
of the Media

LEE EDWARDS

Lee Edwards

Lee Edwards is a senior editor at *The World & I* magazine in Washington, D.C., an adjunct professor of politics at Catholic University, and a senior fellow at The Heritage Foundation. Prior to editing this volume, he authored eleven books, including *The Conservative Revolution: The Movement That Remade America*.

Every leader of the world recognizes the ability of the news media to affect and even transform the politics of his nation. As Russian Nobel laureate Alexander Solzhenitsyn said in his Harvard commencement address, "The press has become the greatest power within the Western countries, more powerful than the legislature, the executive, and the judiciary." Even the mightiest leader is not immune to the power of the press, as the resignation of Richard Nixon (following the Watergate exposés by the *Washington Post*'s Woodward and Bernstein) and the impeachment of Bill Clinton (following the front-page Whitewater articles by the *Washington Times*'s Jerry Seper, which precipitated the Paula Jones and Monica Lewinsky sexual harassment case) attest.

The media have become, in fact, an element of national power, as critical as national resources, economic strength, military might, and political will. Indeed, in our information age, all other components of national power depend upon the media for much of their effectiveness. Whether a nation is drilling for oil or natural gas, caring for the public welfare, selling stocks and bonds, testing a new weapon, or announcing a new law, it must consider the role of the media. For example, one of Ronald Reagan's most memorable addresses was delivered in Normandy on the fortieth anniversary of D-Day. When the site of the Omaha Beach Memorial overlooking the water at Pointe du Hoc was selected, one observer commented that not since the Allies planned the invasion of France in 1944 had the Normandy coast been so carefully inspected.

Abraham Lincoln understood how essential the press is to governance, commenting, "With public sentiment, nothing can fail; without it, nothing can succeed. Consequently he who molds public sentiment, goes deeper than he who enacts statutes or pronounces decisions." Given this power to affect success or failure, the standards of American journalists warrant as much attention as those of lawyers, physicians, business leaders, union leaders, military leaders, or academicians. It will not suffice for journalists to glibly promise fairness, balance, and accountability. What code or philosophy guides their fairness, ensures their balance, and sustains that accountability, not just to readers, viewers, sources, peers, and employers, but to society?

In his provocative work, *News and the Culture of Lying*, the magazine editor Paul H. Weaver states that liberal democracy "isn't automatic"—it requires a commitment throughout society to classical liberal notions such as individual responsibility and limited government. Weaver praises C-SPAN, the cable public affairs network, for practicing what he calls "constitutional democracy," presenting events without commentary and allowing the viewer to make up his own mind about their importance and relevance.

ABC's Cokie Roberts has urged the mainstream media to do "a better job" of explaining the institutions of government, particularly Congress, to the American public. In the annual Theodore H. White Lecture at Harvard, Roberts argued that "all we have defining us, as a nation, is our commitment to the Constitution and the institutions that it created.... To undermine those institutions is a real recipe for disunion."

Ironically, the American media derive their power from the Constitution. James Madison, Thomas Jefferson, John Adams, and the other founders of the American republic had a classical concept of democracy based on the notion that the power to govern and to decide political issues rested in the people. They believed that citizens can discover and maintain a common good through rational argument and debate. In their view, the media should be the middleman between the government and the governed, playing the role of impartial "gatekeeper, scorekeeper, and watchdog," in the words of the political scientist James Q. Wilson.

The media's central role is guaranteed by the First Amendment to the Constitution, which contains the unprecedented pledge, "Congress shall make no law...abridging the freedom of speech, or of the press." This constitutional assurance makes the American press (the news media in modern parlance) the freest in the world. But the founders expected the press to use its liberty and its power prudently toward the preservation of a constitutional republic.

The First Amendment is not a license to make money, win Pulitzer Prizes, or form a fourth branch of government. It is intended to protect the press from government restraint or censorship. It is there to ensure that the people will receive the information they need to make rational, intelligent decisions about their government and their politics. But that process is not possible when at the very center of the Republic—the nation's capital—there is, in the words of *Washington Times* editor in chief Arnaud de Borchgrave, "a two-party system with a one-party press."

There have always been newspapers in the nation's capital. There have been papers owned by political parties, media barons, and profit-seeking conglomerates. There have been liberal papers, conservative papers, and independent papers. There have been powerful papers that shaped national policy and political careers, and impotent papers that quietly passed away. There have been morning papers and evening papers, broadsheet papers and tabloids, thin dailies that sold for a penny, and fat Sunday papers that cost a dollar. There have always been Washington newspapers because Washington is where the future is decided.

So it had been in the nation's capital for close to two centuries until 1981, when, with the death of the *Washington Star*, the city was left with but one daily newspaper—the *Washington*

Post. In embarrassing contrast, London had nine daily newspapers, Paris, thirteen, Tokyo, four (the Japanese dailies had the highest circulation in the world).

Such a news monopoly mocked the First Amendment and the Founding Fathers' vision of the press as a disinterested provider of reliable information to the people. The city and the nation waited for a large newspaper chain—or an ambitious media baron—to announce it was coming to Washington. But the failure of the *Washington Star*, despite the backing of the media giant Time, Inc., led to hesitation and then a decision by apparently everyone not to enter the lists against the *Post*.

Everyone, that is, but a visionary who had been born some eight thousand miles away in Korea, spoke only limited English, and headed a church famous for conducting mass marriage "blessings" in Asia and around the world. The Reverend Sun Myung Moon, founder and leader of the Unification Church movement, believed that his creating of the *Washington Times* would provide an alternative voice in Washington—a daily newspaper that would, in his words, "protect and defend the freedom of people everywhere." And for the past twenty years, the *Times* has enjoyed the editorial freedom to carry out this vision, becoming one of the most influential newspapers in America.

The *Washington Times* appeared when there was a discernable decline in the quality of the news operations of America's mass media, particularly in television. Over thirty years ago, CBS's Edward R. Murrow, a reluctant Jeremiah, warned that television was headed toward "decadence, escapism and insulation from the realities of the world." The American media's emphasis on, even obsession with, the tawdry and the trivial (only recently modified with the terrorist attacks of September 11, 2001) is deeply troubling. Columnist A. M. Rosenthal, the former executive editor of the *New York Times*, lamented the "exploding movement in newspapers, magazines, and TV toward the specialized form of garbage collection known as gossip."

===============

Many in the American media seem to have made a Faustian bargain, trading long-term trust and integrity for immediate fame and fortune. The television critic Walter Goodman charged that TV coverage of politics has been reduced to "stirring up emotions and shutting down minds." Andrew Lack, the president of NBC News, said bluntly that TV news "wittingly or unwittingly is contributing to the dumbing down of America."

The attitude of American journalists has also changed in the last thirty years. "Cynicism has replaced a necessary skepticism," said the *New York Times*'s William Glaberson, "as the core of American journalism." Media cynicism and negativism have profoundly affected American politics. The University of Michigan reported that public confidence in the federal government fell steadily from 1972 until 1992, with just 12 percent (a little more than one in ten Americans) expressing "great confidence" in the executive branch. Following September 11, the public's confidence in Washington has risen dramatically (some surveys placing it as high as 60 percent), but it took a terrorist attack of unprecedented magnitude and a war against global terrorism to reverse the decades-long trend.

Public confidence in the media has also declined precipitously over the last two decades. According to a 1999 Pew Research Center survey, 58 percent of the public doubts the general accuracy of news reports. Kathleen Hall Jamieson, head of the Annenberg School of Communications at the University of Pennsylvania, warns that "journalists are now creating the coverage that is going to lead to their own destruction. If you cover the world cynically…you invite your readers and viewers to reject journalism as a mode of communication because it must be cynical too."

There is evidence of a journalistic shift in the salutary coverage of September 11 and since, but the pressures on the news media to follow a Hobbesian view ("The life of man [is] solitary, poor, nasty, brutish, and short") are enormous. Reform is complicated by the sprawling, decentralized infrastructure of American journalism—1,500 daily newspapers, 7,500 weekly newspapers, 12,000 magazines, 1,460 commercial and noncommercial TV stations, over 11,000 cable TV systems, 11,000 radio stations, and an estimated 10,000 journalists in Washington alone. The Information Age seems to spawn new media almost every day.

In the last two decades—a hiccup of history—we have witnessed the launching of CNN, the first twenty-four-hour-a-day, all news television network; the birth of *USA Today*, the first megacirculation national paper since World War II; the explosion of talk radio led by Rush Limbaugh; the decline of weekly news magazines into weekly infotainment publications; and the coming of the Internet and with it the idea that every man and woman can be a reporter.

The only constant in the ever changing world of political journalism has been the daily newspaper which continues to play the role of main agenda setter for the other media and for public officials and policymakers in Washington, D.C. As one State Department official put it several years ago, "The first thing we do [each morning] is read the newspaper—*the* newspaper— the *New York Times*." The same thing is said today by Washingtontonians about both of their daily newspapers—the liberal *Washington Post* and the conservative *Washington Times*.

The *Post* has the greater circulation, the larger staff, and more Pulitzer Prizes, but the *Washington Times*, in the words of the staunchly liberal *Washington Monthly*, "focuses on people, motives, and inside plays in a kind of high tabloid style that gets closer to the way that Washington really works." And the way that Washington works is determined in large measure by the way the media cover Washington. It's a fair question: Does a congressional hearing or a presidential press conference or a Pentagon briefing really happen if it does not appear in the *Washington Times* or on CNN?

A modern "revolution" in America's journalism occurred on June 1, 1980, when a flamboyant Atlanta businessman started

CNN (the Cable News Network), which influenced U.S. and world politics more than any other media institution in the late twentieth century. Ted Turner intuited that there was a sizeable market at home and abroad for a twenty-four-hour-a-day news service that charged a modest monthly fee. Ridiculed by the old-line broadcast networks and plagued by amateurish production and programming, CNN at first suffered heavy financial losses that almost forced Turner to shut down his perpetual news machine. "We have depended on the news to do our producing for us," wrote a CNN executive after substantial losses in 1984. "When the news is dramatic and compelling, CNN is. When the news is not, CNN is not."

Over the next several years, however, CNN became markedly more professional and its ratings dramatically improved with the rise to power of the telegenic Mikhail Gorbachev in the Soviet Union, the controversial Iran-contra affair, the dramatic Reagan-Gorbachev summits, the 1988 national political conventions which CNN carried gavel-to-gavel (a service once provided by the broadcast networks), the Tiananmen Square demonstrations, and the historic collapse of communism in Eastern and Central Europe. CNN earned an estimated $134 million in 1989 and even more in 1992, confirming that it was no longer the plaything of an eccentric entrepreneur, but a media organization with which to be reckoned.

Possessed of an enormous ego, Turner played to the egos of members of Congress by installing a satellite dish on top of the House of Representatives and running cable to every member's

office. Politicians soon realized they had a greater opportunity of appearing on Turner's twenty-four-hour-a-day channel than the traditional broadcast networks. CNN also gave relatively unknown journalists the chance to become stars; among those who signed up were Bernard Shaw, Lou Dobbs, Christiane Amanpour, Pat Buchanan, and a very young Katie Couric.

CNN became a world-class news organization in 1991 with the Persian Gulf War. With its saturation and on-the-spot coverage, the network almost owned the story. "The best reporting that I've seen on what happened in Baghdad," commented then Defense secretary Dick Cheney, "was on CNN." With exclusive pictures of the allied bombing from atop the Rashid Hotel, CNN was able to increase its American audience to an all-time high, averaging 1.6 million viewers every quarter hour.

In recent years, however, CNN has lost its advantage, due to new competition from MSNBC and the Fox News Channel and a tighter operations budget imposed by its new corporate owner, AOL Time Warner. Still, CNN was the first news channel that millions of Americans turned to on September 11, 2001, and the network earned high ratings for its intensive coverage of the war against terrorism in Afghanistan. Today, CNN reaches eighty-one million households out of a total of about 104 million households in America. MSNBC, started in 1995, is in sixty-one million households while Fox, established in 1996, reaches fifty-seven million households.

When CNN was being launched, the volatile Ted Turner visited the editors of the *New York Times* and boasted, "Don't you know we are going to bury you?" Turner was wrong about the *Times*, which remains America's best and most comprehensive newspaper, but CNN has made a permanent difference in American journalism.

Another significant player in political journalism is C-SPAN, which began in 1979 by presenting the sessions of the U.S. House of Representatives with a staff of only four (including its redoubtable president, Brian Lamb) and a budget of $400,000. Almost a quarter of a century later, C-SPAN is a twenty-four-hour-a-day cable service with two channels that offer not only coverage of the House, the Senate, and congressional hearings, but almost every public affairs event of consequence in Washington,

D.C., plus call-in shows featuring members of Congress and prominent journalists and forty-eight hours of "Book TV" on the weekends. With an annual budget of over $32 million, C-SPAN is must-viewing for people serious about politics and government. Its programming is available to seventy-seven million households via nearly 6,500 cable systems.

The network's audience, according to Lamb, "is the political infrastructure of the country.... It includes everyone from a city councilor, or a university professor, or a reporter who works for a local paper, to elected officials at the local, state, and federal levels, and to corporate executives concerned with issues that affect their businesses." Efforts similar to C-SPAN have been started in several states, including Florida, Massachusetts, New York, and North Carolina. Most of these broadcasts convey the activities of state legislatures directly to the public.

———————

Many middle Americans who feel left out or who are alienated by what they call the "elite" media, like National Public Radio and the New York City-based commercial TV networks, have found a happy, if noisy, home in talk radio. Talk radio became politically important in 1987 when the Federal Communications Commission eliminated the "fairness doctrine." Until then, national talk radio had been usually limited to late nights—and low ratings—when personalities like Larry King conducted lively but noncontroversial conversations with celebrities and sometimes politicians. But when the Reagan administration lifted the regulations requiring radio and TV programs to be balanced politically, "the lid was ripped off the talk."

At the same time, new satellite technology enabled radio producers to beam, and stations to receive, talk shows across the country. This technical development coincided with FM replacing AM as the dominant source of music for listeners. AM radio stations had to come up with a new format to survive. Millions of people began talking and listening and connecting. "I think that talk radio functions," says David Brudnoy, a Boston-based talk show host, "as the last neighborhood in town."

The reigning "king" of the neighborhood is conservative Rush Limbaugh, whose three-hour, Monday-through-Friday afternoon program is heard weekly by an estimated twenty million listeners. Limbaugh's daily critiques of the Clinton administration and his calls for support of the Republicans' Contract with America are credited with helping to bring about the historic GOP capture of Congress in 1994. Michael Harrison, editor and publisher of *Talkers* magazine, argues that talk radio "doesn't create the public's mood; it reflects it."

Whether Limbaugh and his many conservative imitators lead or follow their audience, no one in Washington disputes that talk radio has become a major influence in national politics, loud proof of the people's deep dissatisfaction with politics and journalism as usual. Although highly critical of TV and radio talk shows, media reporter Howard Kurtz of the *Washington Post* concedes that the programs "spur a national conversation, offer a voice to the powerless, [and] provide an outlet for anger and frustration."

And then there is the most recent communications phenomenon—the Internet. The Internet is not as new as many assume, having been established in 1969 at the University of California for purposes of national defense. Private online services began in the 1970s, with CompuServe the first to offer online access service to customers late in the decade. With the introduction of the World Wide Web in the mid-1990s, a network of private providers became the backbone of the Internet.

The newest medium is different from the old media in that Internet users can send and receive messages instantly. The Net is, in fact, a multimedium, integrating text, audio, and visual presentations on the same site. And it may be the fastest growing medium in mass communications history: it took the telephone thirty-eight years to reach a market penetration of 30 percent of households, something the Internet did in seven years. In early 1993, about ninety thousand Americans had access to the Internet; at the end of 2001, the figure was over one hundred million.

After some initial hesitation, old-line media organizations began using the Internet to expand their audiences, particularly among younger Americans. By early 1997, nearly all daily newspapers had electronic issues, including major papers such as the *New York Times*, the *Washington Post*, and the *Washington Times*. C-SPAN has put its broadcast programs on its home page; talk radio is available through Internet sites; CNN and Fox News invite their viewers to email their questions and comments. By

1998, according to Richard Davis, 93 percent of news organizations were using the Internet to gather news, while 86 percent of journalists said they used the Net to find sources. Beyond question, the Internet has ratcheted up the already swift process of news gathering and delivery—every news organization now faces "the challenge of twenty-four-hour news updating."

The pressure to be first coupled with a determination not to be left behind can result in what the political scientist Larry Sabato calls a "feeding frenzy," as it did in January 1998. *Newsweek* had been preparing a long story about the sexual relationship between President Bill Clinton and a young White House intern named Monica Lewinsky, and decided to delay the article for a week, seeking additional verification. Someone from *Newsweek*, leaking with the same sense of purpose as a government official outraged by a possible cover-up of a department scandal, called an Internet columnist named Matt Drudge (who wears an old-fashioned Walter Winchell fedora and operates in much the same fashion as the influential gossip columnist of the 1940s). Drudge immediately went online with a "World Exclusive!"—*Newsweek* was sitting on an article about a relationship between the president and a White House intern.

Instantaneously, in the words of author Richard Reeves, "the nation was wading through minute-to-minute multimedia reportage" of rumors, oaths, affidavits, and depositions, melding traditional journalism and Internet technology. The result of this uneasy marriage was the impeachment, but not the conviction, of President Clinton for perjury and obstruction of justice.

The *Washington Times* did not need Drudge or the Internet to inform its readers about the suspect morality of President Clinton. On July 30, 1991, nearly seven years before the Lewinsky story broke, the *Times* published a front-page story from Little Rock, Arkansas, about Governor Clinton's alleged extramarital affairs, including one with Gennifer Flowers. There was much clucking and tut-tutting among the Washington media. The liberal *New Republic* deplored the news media's "slow slide toward undiscriminating prurience" while conservative columnist George Will sided with Clinton who told reporters his private life was "none of your business." But the 1991 *Times* articles had it right, establishing a correlation between Clinton's private and public behavior.

Most elected officials have integrated the Internet into their offices and campaigns. Every U.S. senator and more than half the members of the House of Representatives have Web pages. Every major presidential contender in 2000 had his own page. John McCain, for example, raised $6.4 million through his Web site and also enlisted an estimated 142,000 volunteer workers. Thirty-one percent of the contributors said they had never before given to a political candidate.

Only half of U.S. households, however, have a personal computer, and Internet users, especially those who use the Net for political news and information, are so far not representative of the general population. Internet users tend to have higher incomes and more education and, according to a Pew Research Center survey, to be more politically active. As a practical matter, says media analyst Bruce M. Owen, "using the Internet is far from being as cheap, easy, and reliable as watching TV."

But as we have seen, television is no longer the reliable news source of old. The tabloidization of television (with the notable exception of PBS's *NewsHour with Jim Lehrer*) was well advanced by the mid-1990s. The news programs were full of names like Joey Buttafucco, Lorena Bobbit, Heidi Fleiss, Woody Allen, and Michael Jackson, all of whom would have been brief footnotes in an earlier era. Television's willingness to dumb down the news was affirmed in the summer of 2001 with the endless items about U.S. representative Gary Condit and Washington intern Chandra Levy, who filled the space once occupied by Monica Lewinsky. Which leads us, once again, to the fact that the daily newspaper remains the most reliable and objective news source in the tidal wave of information inundating the public.

Although the number of daily newspapers in America has declined to less than 1,500, two new ones appeared twenty years ago and have become among the most influential and most quoted in the country—*USA Today* and the *Washington Times*. *USA Today*, like CNN, was the idea of an egotistical media guru— Al Neuharth of Gannett. Started in September 1982, the paper was aimed at younger, affluent Americans who wanted their news short, simple, and fair. The paper was filled with full-color photos and imaginative maps, and the stories did not jump from page to page as in most dailies. Its four sections were titled "News,"

"Money," "Sports," and "Life"—the things that mattered most to most Americans. Critics called it the "McPaper," an embarrassing example of junk food journalism, and predicted—as they did with CNN—that it would fail.

When *USA Today* lost $458 million in its first four years, the skeptics appeared to be right. But thanks to Gannett's deep pockets (it is one of the most profitable media conglomerates in the country), Neuharth's determination to stay the course, and the cooperation of thousands of hotels that pushed the paper under the doors of their guests, *USA Today* became the paper of choice for the American businessman on the go. Today it has a daily circulation of 2.3 million, second only to the *Wall Street Journal*, and its frequent polls of politics and society are among the most cited.

There had always been at least two and sometimes as many as half-a-dozen daily newspapers in Washington, D.C., since the federal government moved to Washington in 1800. But in the summer of 1981, following the closing down of the *Washington Star*, there was only one—the liberal *Washington Post*, whose reservations about President Ronald Reagan were so ingrained that it once placed on its front page three stories about "victims" of the Reagan administration and its policies.

Surely, surmised the experts, someone would come forward and challenge the *Post*'s exclusive control of what Washington policymakers read first thing every morning. True, the *New York Times* delivered a few thousand copies to the nation's capital, but the *Post* blanketed metropolitan Washington with 750,000 copies daily and almost double that on Sunday.

The city and the nation waited for a newspaper chain like Knight Ridder or an ambitious media baron like Rupert Murdoch or an established publication like the *New York Times* or the *Los Angeles Times*—or even a conservative billionaire—to announce that he was coming to Washington. But no one stepped forward until the Reverend Sun Myung Moon. Imprisoned by the Communists as a young missionary, Reverend Moon promised that the paper would be antitotalitarian and profamily, building on America's Judeo-Christian heritage. It would promote unity among all races, nationalities, and cultures. It would help build "the foundation for a lasting world of peace and harmony." These were hardly controversial or exceptional objectives, but when, in the early fall of 1981, representatives of the new journalistic enterprise leased offices in the National Press Building, the reaction of some Washingtonians was so violent that one might have thought that the nation's capital was being invaded by a horde of Visigoths.

One local magazine fulminated, "The Moon Menace Comes to Town!" *The Economist* was skeptical that a "Moonie" paper could compete with the *Post* when a "good" newspaper like the *Washington Star* could not. The *Post* contented itself by quoting "many" but unnamed sources who were certain that the new paper "would be little more than a propaganda sheet for Moon and his church."

The charges were immediately met by Dr. Bo Hi Pak, the first president of the *Washington Times*, who explained that what was needed in Washington was a newspaper that would not "bend the truth toward the right" but provide "the balance so obviously lacking in many major newspapers." Dr. Pak and his associates emphasized that their purpose was to establish a newspaper that had a broad respect for faith, family, and the traditions that had guided mankind through the centuries.

They realized that publication of a major metropolitan daily would be an expensive undertaking. Profit, they said, was not "a primary motivation"—they expected that the paper would have to be "subsidized" for some time to come. And they met the question of editorial control head on, promising that editorial operations would enjoy the same degree of freedom as in any major city newspaper.

Washington journalists took Dr. Pak and his colleagues at their word, and began filling the newsroom and the editorial offices of the new paper. James Whalen, the respected, blunt-talking editor of the *Sacramento Union*, became the *Times*'s editor in chief. Joining him were Smith Hempstone, a former associate editor of the *Washington Star*, who would later succeed Whalen as editor in chief; Philip Evans, former managing editor of the *Philadelphia Bulletin*; and Anne Crutcher, a former editorial writer and columnist for the *Star*. "I've rarely had such freedom," said veteran investigative reporter Gene Goltz, a Pulitzer Prize winner. "It's a delight not to be leaned on by editors who want to write your story for you." Among the many experienced reporters was Jeremiah O'Leary, who had covered every president since Franklin D. Roosevelt. As the *Times*'s White House correspondent, O'Leary frequently bested the opposition by obtaining exclusive interviews with President Reagan and his successor, President George Bush.

On the paper's first anniversary, C.T. Hanson wrote in the *Columbia Journalism Review* that the *Times* was a polished product that could already be ranked among the top fifteen or twenty newspapers in the country. Fred Barnes, writing in the *Washington Journalism Review*, described the *Times* as a throwback to an earlier style of "objective reporting" without embellishment or interpretation. Even the *Post* was obliged to conclude that the *Times* was "a colorful, well-illustrated newspaper" that offered "strait-laced national reporting, a lively feature section called Capital Life ... and a zealous, uncompromising commitment to conservative principles on the editorial and commentary pages."

"I read it every day," admitted Jack Nelson, Washington bureau chief of the *Los Angeles Times*, "and I think a lot of other people do, because it's a good source of information."

From the beginning, the *Washington Times* received steady financial support from its publisher, News World Communications, Inc. Start-up efforts included conversion of an old warehouse on the outskirts of town into a modern headquarters with a computerized, atrium-style newsroom, and a chandeliered ballroom for the high society events on which Washington thrives.

About one thousand people were eventually hired, including 205 reporters and editors, who were paid well—although not as well as rumored. A middle-level reporter earned about $26,000 in 1984.

Since its founding in 1982 by Reverend Moon, the *Washington Times* has provided a vital alternative source of news to what the *Times*'s third editor in chief, *Newsweek* veteran Arnaud de Borchgrave, calls the "dominant media culture." Along the way, the paper has had many scoops and exclusives and received annual journalism prizes and commendations. It is one of the most quoted newspapers in Washington by journalists and politicians—on a circulation of never more than 125,000, one-sixth that of the rival *Washington Post*.

Despite its relatively small circulation, the *Washington Times* has made a measurable difference in the nation's capital and beyond. In 1981, pointed out de Borchgrave, the nation's one-newspaper capital was "a total perversion of what our Founding Fathers intended." Executive editor Woody West explained that the *Times* put an emphasis on fundamentals. "We were trying to put out the kind of newspaper that a lot of kids brought up on Woodward and Bernstein and 'advocacy journalism' had never heard of." Here are some examples of how the *Times* has shaped Washington politics and journalism in the last two decades:

Starting in 1983, the *Times* diligently covered the Strategic Defense Initiative (SDI) in news stories, and steadfastly supported it with editorials and op-ed articles, while the *New York Times*, the *Washington Post*, and other establishment media were skeptical and dismissive. We subsequently learned from Soviet sources in the Politboro and elsewhere that it was SDI , more than any other weapons system, that convinced Moscow it could not win an arms race with the United States and persuaded the Soviets to sue for peace and end the Cold War without firing a shot. As Alexander Solzhenitsyn said, Gorbachev "had no choice but to disarm."

In the mid-1980s, the *Times* perceived the real threat of the Sandinistas and consistently backed Nicaragua's freedom fighters—the contras—as when editor in chief de Borchgrave announced in a front-page editorial the formation of a non-profit corporation to raise $14 million for the contras. The *Times* pledged $100,000 toward the fund after the Democratic House of Representatives voted down a $14 million appropriation for the forces resisting the Marxist Sandinistas. The *Times*'s position was proven correct in 1990 with the election of anti-Sandinista presidential candidate Violetta Chamorro.

Under editor in chief Wesley Pruden, who succeeded de Borchgrave in August 1992, the *Times*'s motto has been "Get it first and get it right," without regard for the political affiliation of the individuals and institutions involved. The paper's bipartisan exposés written from 1989 through 1993 by reporters Paul Rodriguez, George Archibald, and others shook official Washington. The miscreants included Democratic congressman Barney Frank, who used the House gym for homosexual assignations; the House Banking Committee and House Post Office Committee scandals concerning the illegal use of postage and other money; Republican congressman Newt Gingrich, who

used his office and staff to author a book; and Republican senator David Durenberger, who used government funds to pay for his condominium.

One *Times* banner headline about the bad check writing by members of Congress read: "303 Named in Rubbergate." The headline was used extensively in 1992 campaign ads against incumbents from both political parties. The scandals helped trigger the biggest turnover in House membership since World War II—the new House had 110 new members. Howard Kurtz, the *Washington Post*'s media reporter, wrote that the *Times* had broken "important" stories by "digging into scandals at the House Bank and House Post Office well before the rest of the press caught on." One of those that caught on belatedly was the *Post*. The *Post*'s ombudsman, Richard Harwood, was so upset by his paper's poor performance that he wrote a column titled, "Smug and Scoopless."

In the late 1980s and early 1990s, the star of the *Times*'s commentary pages was columnist-economist Warren Brookes, who was the first national writer to question the "danger" of acid rain, to debunk the Massachusetts economic "miracle"—a keynote of Michael Dukakis's 1988 presidential campaign—and to predict that President George H. W. Bush's tax hike in 1990 would lead to his defeat in 1992. Under editor Mary Lou Forbes, a Pulitzer Prize-winner for her coverage of desegregation as a *Washington Star* reporter, the commentary section has become must reading in Washington. Nationally acclaimed writers like Thomas Sowell, Cal Thomas, Nat Hentoff, Georgie Anne Geyer, John Leo, A. M. Rosenthal, Oliver North, and L. Brent Bozell appear and are quoted regularly by C-SPAN on its "Washington Journal" morning program and by talk radio hosts.

When almost every other news organization in America was ignoring Bill Clinton's checkered financial past, the *Times* assigned Jerry Seper, its best investigative reporter, to uncover the facts. In December 1993, Seper revealed that files had been taken from White House counsel Vince Foster's office after his questionable death. Within two weeks, and in response to demands from the *New York Times* and other establishment media, President Clinton agreed to the appointment of an independent counsel to investigate Whitewater, the Arkansas land deal in which Foster was involved as legal counsel. The work of the counsel over the next five years led to Ken Starr's report and Clinton's impeachment.

The *Times* may have set a Guinness record by printing almost four hundred stories about Whitewater, most of them by Seper, who received the Barnet Nover Award for his Whitewater coverage at the 1995 White House Correspondents' Association dinner. "Like it or not," *MediaWeek* said, "the *Washington Times* has become a paper to reckon with." Commenting on the *Times*'s critical but nonpartisan coverage of President Clinton and House Speaker Newt Gingrich, the media watchdog journal, the *Columbia Journalism Review*, wrote: "Washington needs the *Times* . . . to provide diversity and keep the big guys on their toes."

While the Clinton administration was looking the other way, *Washington Times* reporter Bill Gertz reported in 1996 that China was sending missile technology to Syria and Iran and nuclear weapons technology to Pakistan in violation of Beijing's 1994 pledge it would not make such shipments in exchange for America's lifting of trade sanctions. Another series of articles by Gertz detailed how the Clinton administration courted China while the People's Liberation Army were stealing U.S. military technology.

James Woolsey, former director of the Central Intelligence Agency, admitted that as head of intelligence, he had been driven "crazy" by Gertz because he couldn't figure out where the leaks were coming from. "Now," Woolsey said, "I read him religiously to find out what's going on."

Gertz's exclusive stories on nuclear proliferation, commented the *Weekly Standard*, "almost single-handedly" forced the Clinton administration and the Congress to subject China to closer scrutiny. The *New York Times Sunday Magazine* described Gertz as the "most influential reporter" on national security affairs in Washington.

Beginning in 1991, the *Times* strongly endorsed the idea of sexual abstinence education through its editorials and columns, and devoted significant news coverage to the topic. The notion of encouraging abstinence by teenagers was scoffed at by many educators as unrealistic, and the suggestion that it should be taught in middle and high schools was balked at by radical civil libertarians as "religious" education. But the number of young Americans who opted for abstinence and virginity over sexual promiscuity grew steadily throughout the 1990s and into the early 2000s. Other news media, inside and outside Washington, grew to depend upon the *Times*'s in-depth coverage of cultural trends.

Reporter Cheryl Wetzstein, for example, wrote in 1996 that gang members from Hartford, Connecticut, led by "Big Bird" and "Bookman," had turned their lives around through a faith-based approach to work and education. Their religious conversion was reprinted in many newspapers and was given to hundreds of inmates in Connecticut prisons because the former gang members were so well known.

When Promise Keepers in 1997 began attracting as many as 2.5 million men to stadium rallies at which the men rededicated themselves to God, their marriages, and their children, the *Washington Times* provided extensive news and editorial coverage. As columnist Heather Higgins pointed out, Promise Keepers "is a testament to the effectiveness and importance of religion, properly applied, in the public square." Another reflection of the *Times*'s abiding interest in the Culture War was the launching in 1997 of "Family Times," a weekly feature section full of advice, features, and information for families, including columns by James Dobson, founder of the organization Focus on the Family, and physician T. Berry Brazelton. In January 2002, for example, "Family Times" explained how to teach children the rules of personal safety to avoid sexual exploitation or abduction. It is a serious problem: about 3,900 nonfamily abductions occur annually and 114,600 more are attempted.

Such journalism reflected the vision of Reverend Moon, who said on the tenth anniversary of the *Washington Times* that "we cannot relax just because the fight with Communism is ended." The challenges of the next decade, he declared, would be even more difficult as the *Times* highlighted those seeking "to build a moral America, a better world for our children."

"We cover stories," says Pruden, "that other papers are loathe to cover." Many major newspapers, he adds, "have gotten so far from mainstream America that they're no longer aware of what mainstream America is all about." Asked to explain the paper's philosophy, Pruden responds that the *Times* carefully separates commentary and news. Conceding an "aggressive" point of view in the editorials, Pruden argues that "we have tried to keep the news columns as free from bias as possible and on the whole I think we have succeeded."

Although only twenty years old, the *Washington Times* has consistently followed a philosophy outlined over two hundred years ago by *the* founder of the Republic, George Washington. Throughout his career, our *pater patria* maintained that the inalienable rights that Americans enjoyed required a commitment to moral duty and civic virtue. And a crucial aid to the achievement of those objectives, he wrote, was "periodical Publications." Washington declared: "I consider such easy vehicles of knowledge, more happily calculated than any other, to preserve the liberty, stimulate the industry, and meliorate the morals of an enlightened and free people."

Such publications, like the *Washington Times*, reject instant analysis and sound bite-journalism. They do not pander to the prurient. They admit their mistakes quickly and publicly. Conscious of their power, they honor accountability and practice responsibility. They turn for guidance to philosophers like Lord Acton, who stated that "liberty is not the freedom to do what you wish; it is the freedom to do what you ought."

========

There is evidence, particularly since September 11, that more of the media are consciously seeking to play the role envisioned by the Founding Fathers—to be a responsible source of information to the people and an impartial watchdog over government. Carrying out that function, essential to liberal democracy, the media are subjected to their greatest test in wartime.

When a nation is at war, the historian Loren B. Thompson has written, "the military imperative to maintain secrecy and the journalistic imperative to convey truth will always be in tension." So it has been throughout American history. During the Civil War, Secretary of War Edwin M. Stanton ordered a reporter for the *New York Tribune* to be shot for refusing to hand over a dispatch. The reporter was spared when other cabinet members—and President Lincoln—argued for a more lenient policy, declaring that the support of the press was essential to the war effort.

Despite inconsistent censorship, often hostile commanders, and a multifront war, reporters established a new standard for wartime journalism that would influence the reporting of all future conflicts. The questions that confronted the government and the press in the Civil War have resurfaced in every succeeding conflict. What is the proper role of the journalist in wartime? Should he always be an impartial observer, without regard for the consequences of his dispatches? Or does he have a duty to society not to report everything he sees and hears? What are the obligations of the government to help the journalist carry out his job? What are the government's responsibilities to the people? What kind of censorship should there be—voluntary, mandatory, or some combination of the two?

In many ways, World War I created the system of news coverage that prevails today. Modern techniques of communication transmitted stories. The "pooling" of correspondents (allowing a small group of reporters to cover an event and to share their observations with the rest of the press corps) became standard procedure. Government censorship was institutionalized. The press generally cooperated because there had been a formal declaration of war by Congress.

World War II was the first global conflict to employ mass communications as a means of public persuasion and propaganda, for military instruction and education, and as weapons themselves. The radio service of the British Broadcasting Corporation, for example, strengthened English resistance to Nazi Germany's nightly air raids during the Battle of Britain. In France, Holland, and Denmark, underground newspapers and broadcasters sprang up, with writers like Jean Paul Sartre and Albert Camus fighting a propaganda war in tandem with the military resistance.

In the United States, the Roosevelt administration asked journalists to enlist in the war effort, and an overwhelming majority agreed, making possible, as in World War I, a system of voluntary censorship. The consensus was so universal that few of the 2,600 accredited correspondents protested against review of their copy. Journalists of that generation—the so-called "Greatest Generation"—were part of the American mainstream, staunch defenders of liberal democracy and market capitalism. They acknowledged the serious threat of fascist tyranny and the high stakes of the war, and they reported responsibly.

The sense of shared purpose that suffused military-media relations during World War II did not prevail in the Korean War, only five years later, because there was never a formal declaration of war by the United States against North Korea. President Truman worked through the United Nations, which condemned North Korea's aggression in June 1950 and asked U.S. forces to help South Korea repel the invasion. Douglas MacArthur, the U.S. commander in Korea, initially depended upon a voluntary system of censorship like that used in World War II. But after numerous disagreements, a more formal approach was adopted—dispatches were often delayed or heavily censored.

Like Korea, Vietnam was a limited war, without official sanction by Congress, except for the Tonkin Gulf Resolution of August 1964. President Lyndon B. Johnson tried to enlist the media as his mentor Franklin D. Roosevelt had done during World War II. Most of the U.S. news media (which had almost unlimited freedom to report what they wanted) supported the stated goals of the Vietnam conflict—preventing the communist takeover of South Vietnam and thus blocking any domino effect in the rest of Southeast Asia—until the surprising Tet offensive of January 1968.

The enormous impact of Tet was summed up by a gloomy Walter Cronkite in a CBS television special in February: "It is increasingly clear to this reporter that the only rational way out ... [is] to negotiate, not as victors, but as an honorable people who lived up to their pledge to defend democracy, and did the best they could." It should be noted that Cronkite viewed the conflict as a legitimate struggle for democracy and not an imperialist war, as critics then and revisionist historians since have described the Vietnam War. For Cronkite, Vietnam was a just war—but one America could not win.

News coverage of the Vietnam War differed from that of previous conflicts in two important ways: (1) television brought the often bloody war into the living rooms of Americans; and (2) journalists were allowed to travel throughout the country without a military escort and to report whatever they saw as long as it did not disclose militarily sensitive information. No important secrets were revealed, but many correspondents gave highly negative assessments of the U.S. military's performance, producing bitter debates about "Who lost Vietnam?"—the military or the media—that have persisted to this day. The television critic Tom Shales argues that the media coverage of the war had a lasting cultural impact on America, that, in fact, "Vietnam made us a television nation." During the two world wars and the Korean War, the mass media, led by the press, provided news and information, serving as a mediating institution between the public and their government. There was time to consider what had happened, to place the event in its proper context in life and society. But during the Vietnam years, Americans watched the war in their homes as it happened. Reflection became difficult, and then impossible.

Americans made up their minds immediately about the significance of events, with help from an increasingly confrontational media corps, which abandoned the role of mediator for that of advocate. Under the media's guidance, the war was transformed from a necessary—even noble—defense of freedom into an unnecessary involvement in someone else's civil war. The military was determined not to make the same mistake—allowing the media too much freedom in the next war.

On the evening of January 16, 1991, in prime time, a U.S.-led military coalition hit targets in Iraq and Kuwait, initiating the six-week Persian Gulf War. The U.S. military waged a two-front war—one against Iraq's armed forces and a second to enlist the media in support of the war effort. Remembering the bitter fruit of unrestrained media coverage in Vietnam, the Pentagon laid down strict guidelines that required print and broadcast reporters to work in pools, to be accompanied by information officers when in the field, and to submit their copy to military editors.

The Pentagon's spokesman explained that the rules were needed because a small army of eight hundred journalists was in Saudi Arabia demanding to cover the war from the front lines, a logistical impossibility. The media strongly protested the new guidelines, but a national poll showed that nearly eight out of ten Americans supported the Defense Department's restrictions. In fact, almost six in ten surveyed said the military should exert "more control" over the media.

The wide gap between the media and the public regarding war news suggests that the public, following months-long congressional debate and then approval of Operation Desert Storm, firmly supported the Persian Gulf War, as they did World War II, while many in the media adopted a negative stance, as in the latter days of the Vietnam War. The public accepted that in a war, when the lives of individual soldiers as well as national security are at stake, a free press can be legitimately, if reasonably, restricted. They expected the mass media to acknowledge their power to affect the course of a conflict and to accept responsibility for their actions and their mistakes, if any.

The American public's concern about the conduct of the media in the Gulf War was heightened when on several occasions American reporters provided tactical intelligence about the conflict not only to the viewing public but to the enemy. On the first night of the war, a CBS cameraman traveling between Khafji and the border with Kuwait told anchorman Dan Rather on the air that there were no Saudi troops between his position and the border and that the Iraqis could "just walk in there...if they wanted." Apparently, the Iraqis were listening, because the battle for Khafji followed.

A turning point in war journalism, wrote the media critic John Corry, had been reached: the old ideal of objectivity was replaced by a new standard of "neutrality" by which a reporter stood midway between two opposing sides, even when one of the sides was his own country. CBS's Mike Wallace had said, at a 1987 conference on the military and the press, that it would be appropriate for him to accompany enemy troops into battle, even if they ambushed (and presumably killed) American soldiers. During the Gulf War, CNN's Bernard Shaw refused to be debriefed by American officers after he left Baghdad because, he said, reporters must be "neutral."

There was deep irony in Shaw's declaration of neutrality, since he and other modern correspondents are fond of describing Edward R. Murrow as their journalistic model. Yet, in the Battle of Britain and other World War II battles, Murrow made it clear which side he was on. Certainly, he would never have traveled to Berlin, checked into the Grand Hotel, and then reported, without comment, Adolf Hitler's tirades.

The Persian Gulf War heightened the historic struggle over information between the mass media and the military, which do not, after all, have much in common. As the *Washington Post*'s Henry Allen conceded, "When the military makes a mistake in combat, its own people die. When the press makes a mistake, it runs a correction." Although ombudsman Richard Harwood concluded that nothing of significance to the public interest had been suppressed in the war, the Pentagon did adopt, after a year of study, less restrictive war zone rules for journalists, conscious of its responsibility in a democracy to keep the public prudently informed.

Under the one-word banner headline, "INFAMY," *Washington Times* reporter Frank Murray began his September 12, 2001, story: "Suicidal terrorists piloting airplanes hijacked from Dulles and Boston airports toppled the 110-story twin towers of the

World Trade Center and demolished part of the Pentagon yesterday in the worst terrorist attack on American soil." The *New York Times*'s headline was, "U.S. ATTACKED, Hijacked Jets Destroy Twin Towers And Hit Pentagon In Day of Terror." The *Washington Post* headlined, "Terrorists Hijack 4 Airliners, Destroy World Trade Center, Hit Pentagon; Hundreds Dead."

In a crisis, says media scholar Doris Graber, the media perform the following "indispensable" functions: they diffuse vital information to the public and public officials; interpret events, placing them in their proper context; and provide emotional support for troubled and uncertain communities. In the hours and days following the terrorist attack on Tuesday morning, September 11, the news media discharged their responsibilities brilliantly. As the *Weekly Standard*'s Fred Barnes wrote, "the stories were fact-filled, fair, balanced, poignant, comprehensive, and politically neutral." The press, he said, "has been more in sync with the American people since September 11 than at any time in decades." (Even when the U.S. bombing in Afghanistan began a month later and the coverage became more critical, the major complaint of the media seemed to be that the war on terrorism was not being conducted forcefully enough.)

Appearing on the "Late Show with David Letterman," CBS anchorman Dan Rather began crying when the New York City firefighters who had given their lives in the World Trade Center attacks were mentioned. Liberal icon Geraldo Rivera, a stubborn defender of Bill Clinton, quit his CNBC program and joined Fox

342

News Channel to cover the war in Afghanistan. His explanation: "How can you be a dove when someone has committed mass murder in your neighborhood?"

CNN head Walter Isaacson sent a memo to correspondents, instructing them to remind viewers of the terrorist attacks that had prompted America to go to war in Afghanistan. One anomaly was the *New York Times*'s veteran correspondent R. W. Apple Jr., who early on kept finding dire similarities between the U.S. operations in Afghanistan and Vietnam, using the word "quagmire." When the Taliban were defeated in less than three months, media critics waited in vain for Apple to acknowledge his misuse of the word "quagmire."

Responding to the prevailing public mood, the great majority of journalists refrained from running stories that might have damaged the American effort. When the Washington bureau chief of the thirty-two-newspaper Knight Ridder chain learned of the first secret commando operation in Afghanistan in September, he called the Pentagon for comment. An official responded that publication would "endanger the lives of the servicemen involved and compromise any chances of success." The reporter did not hesitate, and declined to publish his certain exclusive.

Forty journalists from seventeen major news organizations were informed in early October of an imminent U.S. attack on the Taliban. There was an implicit understanding, wrote the *Post*'s Howard Kurtz, that the journalists "would keep quiet," and all of them did. At the same time, the Pentagon apologized to the news media in early December for its "severe shortcomings" in helping news organizations to cover military operations in Afghanistan. It promised, publicly, to implement Defense Secretary Donald Rumsfeld's stated press policy of "maximum coverage, minimum hassle." As they had for 150 years, the military and the media were sorting out their obligations to each other and to the public in wartime.

Their task was complicated by the rapid technological changes of the late twentieth and early twenty-first centuries. "Technology has changed the news industry since the Persian Gulf War," wrote *Insight* magazine's J. Michael Waller, "with more 24-hour TV news programming and constant Internet reporting that require steady updates in an intensely competitive environment."

Some critics have argued that journalistic standards have declined, with gossip and unverified information "more readily reported than before." Among the more obvious offenders are the cable news channels with their ticker tape of stories that rolls across the bottom of TV screens. Little context can be given, and the usual impression is that the world will soon be coming to an end. Such news does not serve either the public or policymakers well.

In war or peace, journalists must accept the responsibility of power and believe in the power of responsibility. To help them achieve the right balance between power and responsibility, they would do well to listen to Paul Johnson, British historian, journalist, and valued contributor to this volume, who elsewhere has proposed ten commandments—rules of moral conduct—for all who exercise media influence.

Johnson's first rule is the desire to discover and tell the truth, making it clear to readers and viewers that the truth is not always simple. The second commandment is that journalists should "think through the consequences of what they tell," asking themselves, "What will legitimately inform and what will corrupt?" The third is that truth telling is not enough and can be dangerous without an "informed judgment." Journalists, says Johnson, should always be deepening and broadening their knowledge of the world and its peoples.

The fourth commandment is that men and women of the mass media should have a missionary urge to educate—to tell the public not only what it wants to know but what it needs to know. The fifth commandment (perhaps the most difficult of all) is to distinguish between the reasoned "public opinion" that assures liberal democracy and the transitory phenomenon that is "popular opinion." In a republic, James Madison said in Federalist No. 50, it ought to be the reason, not the passion, of the public that sits in judgment.

The sixth commandment is that the media must show the willingness to lead—to make an unpopular but principled decision—as the *Washington Times* did in the 1980s when it supported SDI and the contras and in the 1990s when it backed abstinence education and the pro-life movement. The seventh commandment is to display courage, which Johnson calls the greatest of all virtues. The eighth commandment is the willingness to admit error. The unforced admission of error demonstrates that a newspaper or a TV network or station has a sense of honor and a conscience.

The ninth commandment is the ability to be habitually fair—to see and tolerate other points of view and to exercise "temperance and restraint in expressing your own." The tenth and last commandment is to respect and honor the intrinsic power of words. As Johnson says, words can enlighten and uplift or they can kill. In today's media environment, when so many journalists are careless about the power of words and compromise their obligations under the First Amendment, the need for traditional gatekeepers like the *Washington Times*, especially in Washington, D.C., the news center of the world, is greater than ever before.

President Ronald Reagan and British prime minister Margaret Thatcher were two pillars of Western democratic ideals whose steeliness helped cause the Kremlin to lose its imperialistic resolve.

The anticommunist implacability of Pope John Paul II, the first Polish pontiff, fueled nationalist sentiments and democratic aspirations in Poland that weakened Moscow's grip on the nation. Here, he visits Monterey, California, in 1987.

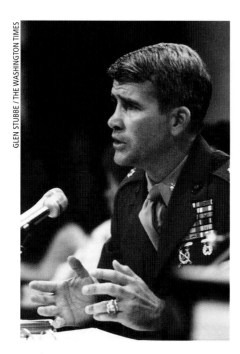

Lieutenant Colonel Oliver North became emblematic of America's profreedom "Reagan doctrine" through his testimony before Congress over funneling arms to Nicaragua's anticommunist contras.

In the 1980s, *Washington Times* editor in chief Arnaud de Borchgrave (right) shook Washington with a front-page editorial announcing a new nonprofit group to raise $14 million for the contras. The *Times* pledged to give $100,000.

Reagan's CIA trained and funded the Afghan freedom fighters, who caused the Soviets to eventually give up and leave the country in 1989.

One potent weapon in the U.S. anticommunist arsenal was a non-military one—airing the democratic truth worldwide through the Voice of America radio network.

The exclusives of *Washington Times* reporters like Bill Gertz have alerted the public time and again to national security threats.

The arrival of Kremlin leader Mikhail Gorbachev (at podium) on the world stage marked a period of inventive but ultimately fruitless maneuvers to save the Soviet system.

Signaling the global trend toward freedom in communist nations, a huge crowd of prodemocracy students gathered in Beijing's Tiananmen Square in 1989—a movement Chinese authorities brutally suppressed.

In Eastern Europe, the profreedom movement was successful. Here, a German youth waves victoriously from atop the Berlin Wall on November 12, 1989, three days after it "fell."

In a journalistic tour de force, *Times* managing editor Josette Shiner in 1994 went to Pyongyang, capital of North Korea, one of the last few communist states on earth, to interview President Kim Il Sung (now dead).

One of the *Times*'s strong suits has been its comprehensive political coverage. Here, former president George H.W. Bush appears at a party convention with his wife, Barbara, Dan and Marilyn Quayle, and actor Arnold Schwarzenegger.

During the 1990s, President Bill Clinton and first lady Hillary Clinton were conservatives' favorite rhetorical target. The president, along with daughter Chelsea, are seen here as his wife practices her swearing-in as New York's junior U.S. senator.

Special prosecutor Kenneth Starr, speaking to the media, spent years probing the Clintons on a spate of ethical and legal issues. The *Times*, especially through correspondent Jerry Seper, led media organizations in its ground-breaking coverage of these issues.

The *Times* provided congressional Republicans, seen here signing the 1994 Contract With America, with front-page coverage they seldom got elsewhere. The Contract helped boost them to a historic success that year.

Federal Reserve chairman Alan Greenspan, testifying on Capitol Hill, made headlines throughout the 1990s for his shrewd stewardship of the U.S. economy.

Vladimir Putin (here with President George W. Bush) became the first Russian president to accomplish a democratically elected transition in the huge Eurasian country.

The rise of Microsoft Corporation, led by Bill Gates (above), was the biggest economic success story of the past two decades.

WHITE HOUSE CONFERENCE
ON CLIMATE CHANGE

The Challenge of Global Warming

VICE PRESIDENT
ALBERT GORE

PRESIDENT
WILLIAM J. CLINTON

The *Times* gave continuing, objective coverage to scientific issues that became intensely politicized, such as the global warming concept.

GERALD HERBERT / THE WASHINGTON TIMES

The collapse of the Twin Towers of New York's World Trade Center galvanized the *Times* and other U.S. media to focus deeply on links between extremist Islam and terrorism.

Following the attack on the Twin Towers, there were anti-American rallies in a number of Muslim nations, as here in Peshawar, Pakistan—but the Islamabad government was unflagging in its support of the U.S. war on terrorism.

GERALD HERBERT / THE WASHINGTON TIMES

Anti-Taliban Afghans exit a Jalalabad compound used by Osama bin Laden's al Qaeda terrorist group, in November 2001 after the city's liberation by mujahideen and U.S. forces.

GERALD HERBERT / THE WASHINGTON TIMES

Times editor in chief Wesley Pruden (center) has guided the paper's coverage since August 1992. Here, he is seen with Secretary of State Colin Powell, columnist Suzanne Fields (standing), and Rep. Jennifer Dunn (R-Washington).

In its coverage of the "Culture War"—a conflict that conservatives see as at least as important as the Cold War—the *Times* spotlighted Tipper Gore, wife of former vice president Al Gore, when she was a vocal critic of crude rock music lyrics.

Former education secretary and drug czar William Bennett, who is also the best-selling author of *The Book of Virtues*, has been a conservative leader on moral issues.

Over the years, the *Times* has focused attention on entrepreneurial and faith-based solutions to urban problems, an approach represented by Robert Woodson, president of the National Center for Neighborhood Enterprise.

Full coverage of traditional values—and threats thereto—has always been a *Times* hallmark. Here, an AIDS Coalition to Unleash Power (ACT UP) demonstrator vents his outrage in 1994 over the Roman Catholic Church's position on homosexuality.

Concern with life issues has also characterized the *Times* over the years. Here, actor Michael J. Fox speaks to a Senate committee in September 2000 in favor of federal funding of embryonic stem cell research. Beside him is actress Mary Tyler Moore.

Italian embryologist Severino Antinori (left) and his colleagues tell the media in August 2001 about their intention to clone a human being.

Two demonstrators have a friendly— but serious—disagreement over abortion at the U.S. Supreme Court building in January 2002.

Tens of thousands of pro-life demonstrators march through the streets of Washington, D.C., in 1984, as they have every January since the high court's 1973 *Roe v. Wade* ruling.

The *Times* has given coverage to nonliberal feminist groups the left-leaning media have ignored. Here, former *New York Times* writer Hilton Kramer speaks at a conference sponsored by one such organization, the Independent Women's Forum.

Education constitutes a major *Times* interest. The paper has given fair and full attention to programs involving government vouchers that allow parents to send their children to schools of their choice, including religious ones. Here, Eric Stearns teaches his class at the IDEA Academy, a public charter school in Washington, D.C.

During its first two decades, the *Times* has provided regular and sensitive coverage of religion issues. Here, President George W. Bush, surrounded by leaders of faith-based charities, signs documents establishing a White House office to disburse government funds to such groups.

Some 50,000 men, seeking to become better and more godly husbands and fathers, join in praying at a Promise Keepers event at RFK Stadium in Washington, D.C.

Times founder Reverend Sun Myung Moon has seen the realization of his vision of a newspaper that would protect and defend the freedom of people everywhere.

The Collapse
of the
Soviet Union

RICHARD PIPES

Richard Pipes

Richard Pipes is the Frank B. Baird Jr. Professor of History Emeritus at Harvard University. A native of Poland, Pipes served as President Reagan's director of East European and Soviet Affairs for the National Security Council. He is the author of numerous books, including *The Russian Revolution* and *Communism: A History.*

he collapse of the communist regime in the USSR and the dissolution of both the Soviet Union and the Soviet Empire ten years ago were, in some respects, events with precedent in history.* In every case that one can think of when two hostile blocs confronted one another—from the Greek-Persian clash to World War II—tension resulted in armed conflict which caused the defeat and often the destruction of one of the contestants. In the case of the so-called "Cold War" which pitted a bloc led by Russia against one headed by the United States, the conflict lasting nearly half a century was resolved without recourse to arms as the former simply imploded. To be sure, there were military engagements and they

---

* The collapse of communism and the dissolution of the Soviet Union, were, strictly speaking, distinct events, separated by nearly one year. Communism fell in Russia in January 1991, when the Supreme Soviet passed the law of "Private Property in the RSFSR" which authorized private enterprise in all branches of the economy. The Soviet Union disintegrated in December of that year.

cost the United States over 100,000 casualties; but they were waged on the communist side by proxy forces and took place on the periphery of both countries. On a couple of occasions the two superpowers seemed on the verge of war but in the end their tensions were peacefully resolved.

It is not far-fetched to assume that the unwillingness of the two blocs to risk war was an unanticipated benefit of nuclear weapons, the very thing that ill-informed opinion feared was certain, sooner or later, to cause the extinction of life on earth. In fact, it had the opposite effect: it preserved lives. The Cold War was a blessing in disguise, since the alternatives to it were either capitulation and the spread of totalitarianism across the globe, or else "hot" war with all its awesome consequences. To call someone a "Cold Warrior" derisively in the sense of "war-monger," therefore, is mindless.

We want to know answers to two central questions: why did communism collapse and why was its fall so unanticipated by both the public at large and "Sovietologists"? We shall attempt to answer them in the following order: As concerns the collapse of the Soviet Union, we will distinguish between internal and external causes. In the first category, emphasis will be placed on fundamental misconceptions of Marxist-Leninist theory which vitiated all efforts to construct a communist society, no matter how ruthless the means employed. This will be followed by a discussion of economic failures that undermined the regime, the centrifugal forces of minority nationalisms, and intellectual dissent. In treating the external factors, we will stress first and foremost the willingness of the United States to meet the challenges of the Cold War flung by Stalin even before World War II had come to an end, singling out the unique contribution of Ronald Reagan who, alone among U.S. presidents, having come to realize that the force driving the USSR to aggression was the nature of the communist regime, committed himself to subverting it. Finally, we will inquire into the puzzling failure of Western specialists on communism to appreciate its weaknesses and anticipate its fall.

Causation presents some of the most troublesome difficulties to anyone engaged in the social sciences, history included, because it occurs on so many different levels, from the fundamental to the haphazard. When we deal with long-term *processes*, such as the rise of capitalism or demographic shifts, the accidental is irrelevant. By contrast, when the subject is an historical *event*, the accidental and the fundamental are inextricably linked and it is virtually impossible to disentangle the one from the other. As a rule, however, it may be argued that the accidental affects more the timing of the event than its nature, the latter of which is determined by underlying factors. Thus, the assassination of Arch Duke Ferdinand in Sarajevo in July 1914 indisputably set off World War I but it may not be said to have "caused" it inasmuch as the preparations for it, military as well as diplomatic, had been underway for decades and hence it was bound to break out sooner or later.

One may disagree whether the collapse of communism was due primarily to internal or external factors, but clearly both played a role. My personal view is that the decisive catalysts were internal but that external influences played a major role in the timing of this event.

The clique of professional revolutionaries who seized power in Russia in October 1917 considered themselves staunch realists and such they were in the choice of means. But in their long-term objectives they were extreme utopians. They dismissed all history along with anthropology, economics, and psychology as so much useless baggage, irrelevant to the world they were determined to construct on the ruins of the past. Marx, they believed, provided them with the key to remaking man and society, and they proceeded to implement his program with a ruthlessness that derived from the conviction that the world as it had existed for thousands of years was but a pale shadow of the world as it could be and as it would be after they had done their job of cleansing it of the legacies of the past.

The magnitude of their utopianism—the conviction that the Revolution would make it possible to bring into being a totally new breed of human beings with unlimited potential—is well illustrated in a passage from Trotsky's *Literature and Revolution*. In the communist future, he promised,

> Man will, at last, begin to harmonize himself in earnest.... He will want to master first the semi-conscious and then also the unconscious processes of his

own organism: breathing, the circulation of blood, digestion, reproduction, and, within the necessary limits, subordinate them to the control of reason and will.... The human species, the sluggish *Homo sapiens*, will once again enter the state of radical reconstruction and become in his own hands the object of the most complex methods of artificial selection and psychophysical training.... Man will make it his goal...to create a higher sociobiological type, a superman, if you will.... Man will become incomparably stronger, wiser, more subtle. His body will become more harmonious, his movements more rhythmic, his voice more melodious.... The average human type will rise to the heights of an Aristotle, Goethe, Marx. And beyond this ridge, other peaks will emerge.

This vision was projected not by an intellectual dreamer but by the ex-commander of the Red Army, a man who once defined the guillotine as a device that "shortens a man by the length of a head," who ordered all White Army officers taken prisoner in the Crimea to be shot, and who introduced Soviet Russia to concentration camps.

In other words, the communist experiment had to succeed or fail to the extent that it managed to produce a "superman," totally in control of himself, indeed, his own maker. This is the longest-term and most fundamental criterion by which communism must be judged because if it could not accomplish a thorough transformation of Homo sapiens, all its other expectations were bound to be frustrated.

The critical human quality that required change was acquis-itiveness. In their *Communist Manifesto* of 1848, Marx and Engels wrote that "the theory of the Communists may be summed up in a single sentence: Abolition of private property." And this was possible in the long run only if humans rid them-selves of their acquisitive impulses: impulses that the founders of communism regarded not as inborn instincts but as habits inculcated by class society.

The objective clearly was not attained. Indeed, the very opposite happened: *Homo sovieticus* turned out to be even more acquisitive than his capitalist counterpart, because goods and services in his society were both much scarcer and less secure. For ordinary citizens, life in such societies turned out to be an unceasing struggle for necessities. Marx had expected to liberate humanity from dependence on material things: true freedom for him meant not civil and political rights—these Engels charac-terized as "sham" freedoms—but emancipation from subjection to material necessity. Only in such a truly "free" community, rid of the desire as well as the need for possessions, would mankind realize its true potential. "In communist society," Marx predicted in *German Ideology*,

> society regulates the general production and thus makes it possible for me to do one thing to-day and another to-morrow, to hunt in the morning, fish in the after-

noon, rear cattle in the evening, criticize after dinner, just as I have in mind, without ever becoming hunter, fisherman, shepherd or critic.

Needless to elaborate, nothing remotely like this ever emerged in the Soviet Union or any other communist country. As early as 1920, Adolf Ioffe, a committed socialist, complained to Trotsky that the whole of Soviet society was permeated with greed:

> From top to bottom and from bottom to the top, it is everywhere the same. On the lowest level, it is a pair of shoes and a soldier's shirt; higher up, an automobile, a railroad car, the dining room of the Council of People's Commissars, quarters in the Kremlin or at the Hotel National; and on the highest rungs, where all this is available, it is prestige, prominence, and fame.

But even had the communists succeeded in eliminating acquisitive impulses in one generation they had no assurance that the generations that followed would not be infected with the same vice. It was essential for them, therefore, to insist, contrary to the teachings of geneticists, that acquired characteristics can be inherited, which is why Stalin supported the Lamarckian "theories" of the charlatan Trofim Lysenko. Here, indeed, was the Achilles' heel of Marxism: for unless the qualities acquired under communist rule by a combination of education and compulsion could be genetically passed on to one's offspring, the regime could never attain stability; it would forever have to teach and coerce, i.e., negate the very freedom which was its ultimate objective.

But there was still another, no less intractable problem with the communist vision. Freedom in its view entailed equality: the abolition of private property was meant, among other things, to eliminate social classes and the exploitation of one class by another. And yet, as it turned out in practice, implied in its premise was the need for inequality.

To deprive people of their belongings and to make sure that they did not reacquire them demanded a coercive apparatus as well as an extensive bureaucracy to manage the requisitioned properties. Theses cadres, made up of human beings with ordinary human impulses, demanded—and received—as a reward for their work goods and services which in an economy of scarcity had to be denied to ordinary mortals. Thus emerged the phenomenon of the *nomenklatura*, a service elite that resembled the tsarist gentry (*dvorianstvo*). It led lives quite separate from the rest of the population, enjoying access to its own shopping facilities, restaurants, hospitals, rest homes and sanatoria, and even cemeteries. Although its status was fully dependent on the good will of the government, in time it became virtually hereditary.

The *nomenklatura* came into being almost immediately after the October 1917 Bolshevik coup and crystallized into a distinct privileged class by the early 1920s, because Stalin, placed in charge of the Party bureaucracy, realized early the advantages he could secure in his drive for power by creating an administrative body dependent on him for the good things in life. Trade union leaders, resentful of this phenomenon, protested in vain: even Lenin, troubled as he was by the emergence of an uncontrollable Soviet bureaucracy, labeled them "the Workers' Opposition" and demanded their expulsion from the party. The *nomenklatura*, therefore, grew by leaps and bounds. By the time the Soviet Union collapsed, it numbered some 750,000 Party members who with their families accounted for 1.5 percent of the population. Their existence was a glaring reproach to the communists' claim that they had created an egalitarian society.

The third fundamental cause of communism's failure was the illusion of workers' international solidarity. Marx claimed that class loyalties cut across national boundaries: just as the capitalists promoted their interests globally, so did labor. The slogan launched by the *Communist Manifesto* and subsequently adopted by the Socialist and Communist Internationals—"Proletarians of all countries, unite!"—articulated this faith. Nationalism, in this view, was a sham ideology, promoted by the bourgeoisie to thwart the global brotherhood of the working class. The workers were said to have no fatherland.

Reality once again turned out to be very different. Industrial workers in countries with advanced social security systems felt loyal to their respective states because they provided them with valuable benefits. In Third World countries, to the extent that they had an industrial working class, the workers felt little if any affinity for their counterparts in industrial countries because they appeared in their eyes as not much better than the imperialist bourgeoisie. In the 1920s, the Tatar communist Sultan Galiev, having observed how Russian workers in the borderlands excluded Muslims from participation in Soviet political institutions, decided that the real class conflict pitted not the workers against the bourgeoisie but industrial nations against under-developed ones—a theory later independently developed by Mao Tse-tung.

That international class loyalty was a myth became glaringly obvious in the summer of 1914 when, despite solemn pledges to the contrary, socialists in virtually every country voted war credits for their respective governments. In 1920, as the Red Army advanced into Poland to "liberate" it from landlords and capitalists, Polish workers and peasants, to Lenin's dismay, sided with the landlords and capitalists against the invaders. During World War II, Stalin exhorted his subjects to fight not for communism but for Mother Russia. And the German invading army, whose manpower consisted of more than one-half communists and socialists, dutifully slaughtered their Soviet class brethren on behalf of an antisocialist and anticommunist racial doctrine.

Nationalist passions also afflicted the communist bloc, beginning with Tito's Yugoslavia and ending with Mao's China. The quarrels between the USSR and China, which at one point almost erupted in armed conflict, centered on the question of which country was the true leader of the world revolutionary movement.

Such are the three most basic causes of communism's ulti-mate collapse: a faulty conception of human nature; the need, in order to enforce equality, to promote inequality; and illusions of international class loyalties. They doomed communism from the outset. The only question was when it would fall: in Russia, its life was prolonged by the application of unrestrained ruthlessness by the government and the legendary endurance of its people.

If we next turn to the middle level of causation where processes are affected not by fundamental considerations, independent of the individual will, but by specific human decisions, the most conclusive factors appear to have been of an economic nature.

With the exception of Leonid Krasin, who played a secondary role in the Soviet government, none of the Bolsheviks had the slightest experience with business: their entire knowledge of economics came from reading the "classics" of Marxism and newspaper accounts of economic mobilization carried out by the belligerent powers during World War I, especially Imperial Germany. Yet this lack of experience did not inhibit them from seizing control of a country with the world's fifth largest economy. Nationalizing over a period of three years all of finance, industry, and transport, they found themselves directly in charge of running on a day-to-day basis enterprises that employed millions. When in 1929–32 they carried out the so-called "collectivization" of agriculture, the entire national economy was in their hands. This fact gave them near total power because it enabled them to determine the livelihood of every citizen by rewarding the loyal and punishing the rest; but it also imbued them with the deceptive feeling that such control made it possible to run the economy in a uniquely rational and productive manner.

Although the visible instrument of political control in communist countries was the ubiquitous security police, its most effective weapon was the monopoly on economic resources. By the 1930s, for all practical purposes every citizen turned into an employee of the state—or, more precisely, the ruling party—which used this power to promote its own interests. The abolition of private property, the defining attribute of communism, thus signified not the complete emancipation of citizens from dependence on material goods, as Marx had anticipated, but, on the contrary, their absolute dependence on the new owner of these goods, the state.

The Bolsheviks understood this fact very well. But they also were convinced that the concentration of all economic assets in their hands made for economic efficiency because it allowed rational allocations of resources and labor that were beyond the reach of economies driven by the quest of profits. They believed in bigness: the bigger the enterprise, the better. This is why, within weeks of seizing power, they formed large-scale cartels administered by the Supreme Economic Council, later renamed the State Planning Commission (Gosplan), "the trust of trusts." In reality, the council failed for a long time to assert control over Soviet finances and industry, and productivity dropped disastrously. This failure could be attributed to the impact of the civil war. The faith in central management never wavered and in time the Gosplan did indeed come to run the Soviet economy.

This arrangement had one single advantage: it permitted giant crash programs such as the construction of vast industrial enterprises or dams. For all their propaganda value, however, such prestigious undertakings unbalanced the economy: unglamorous aspects of the infrastructure were neglected, be they agriculture, storage facilities, or housing.

The centralization of economic decision-making also caused the Soviet Union and other communist regimes to miss out on scientific and technological innovation. The industrial managers plied the safe path, concentrating on products which they knew had fueled the Industrial Revolution in the West, and showing a distinct mistrust of innovation—financed by venture capital in the West. As Yuri Andropov remarked,

An economic planner who would take a "risk" and introduce into the enterprise new technology, who would put to use or invent new equipment, would often turn out to be the loser, whereas he who stays clear of innovation loses nothing.

The most glaring example of such a lag was the Soviet Union's very late entry into the realm of modern information technology which in the late twentieth century revolutionized Western communications, economies, as well as warfare.

Another byproduct of the nationalization of productive assets was the decline of the work ethic. This phenomenon was anticipated two-and-a-half thousand years ago by Aristotle in the dispute with his teacher, the protocommunist Plato, when he wrote in *Politics*: "How immeasurably greater is the pleasure when a man feels a thing to be his own: for surely the love of self is a feeling implanted by nature." Low levels of productivity in societies which abolish private property in the means of production is a fact of such universality as to require no additional proof. In the Soviet Union, the population could physically survive collectivization only because Stalin allowed collective farm households small private plots on which to grow produce for the open market and to raise cattle: this minuscule sector of the economy provided the USSR with a disproportionate quantity of fruits and vegetables, meat and dairy products.

Even so, poverty proved ineradicable. Except for the *nomenklatura*, the citizenry of the USSR suffered a living standard which to westerners was quite incomprehensible. In the mid-1980s, when Gorbachev initiated his reforms, 57 percent of the population lived on the equivalent of ten dollars a month or less while one hundred million citizens had less living space than the prescribed and very modest nine square meters (ninety-seven square feet) per person.

Grinding poverty had serious demographic consequences. Under tsarism, Russia had the highest birth rate in Europe. It persisted until the late 1920s, despite the several catastrophes that had struck the country, including civil war and the famine of 1921–22 which claimed over five million lives. It plunged with collectivization and the terror policies of the 1930s. World War II inflicted enormous human losses on the country. In 1972, the demographic curve stood at one-half of what it had been in 1928. It would have been lower still were it not for the high fertility levels of the country's Muslims. By the mid-1970s Eastern Slavs ceased to reproduce themselves as more Russians and Ukrainians died each year than were born.

All of which created among the Soviet leaders the sense that the country was in deep crisis, masked, at least from foreign eyes, by the global advances of the communists and the Soviet Union's military prowess. From conversations with them one gains the impression that in the 1980s they had concluded things could not go on in the old accustomed ways, that the system had to be thoroughly reformed; and if that proved impossible, then it was ready to be dismantled.

One obvious way of alleviating the economic crisis without major reforms was to curtail sharply military expenditures, which are estimated to have absorbed at least one-quarter and possibly as much as one-third of the country's Gross Domestic Product. Yet this was not a feasible solution. Ever since the failure to spread the revolution to the industrial countries of the West, that is from the early 1920s, the Soviet regime had come to rely on military power to assert its global prominence. Furthermore, to justify its dictatorship, it had become habituated to frightening its population with imaginary foreign threats which required a large military force to repel. After their victory in World War II, the armed forces were the most popular institution in the country. Soviet Russia's pioneering work on intercontinental ballistic missiles earned her immense prestige at home as well as abroad and elevated her to the status of a "superpower" to which she could aspire neither by virtue of her economy nor any other accomplishment. For all these reasons, military appropriations could not be substantially cut back and continued, year after year, to absorb a completely disproportionate share of the nation's meager wealth.

The Soviet system was of a piece: it stood or fell as an entity. No part of it could be altered without fatally subverting the whole. Its monolithic strength was also its weakness. This meant that any tampering with the economic system as established in the first quarter of a century of its existence presented a deadly threat to its survival. The country's leadership in the 1980s thus faced a genuine dilemma: leaving things as they were spelled slow asphyxiation; interfering with them threatened instant death. The leadership delayed making a decision as long as it could and then, when delay was no longer possible, took a chance on reform. As it happened, it brought the whole edifice crashing down.

One of the potentially most explosive issues threatening Soviet domestic stability was the so-called "national question"—a euphemism for what in reality was the question of maintaining an empire in an age when all the other empires had either dissolved or were in the process of dissolving.

In contrast to European empires, which came into being by means of expansion overseas, the Russian Empire emerged as a result of the metropolitan region, Russia, expanding overland. The territorial contiguity of the metropolis and its colonial possessions tended to conceal in some measure the Russian and Soviet states' imperial nature: most Russians, both before and after the Revolution, thought of their country, in which they constituted at most one-half of the population, as another United States, that is, a multinational commonwealth destined over time, through the process of ethnic assimilation, to evolve into a nation-state.

This expectation was unrealistic because unlike the United States, whose population, with the exception of native Indians and one time slaves, consisted exclusively of people who had voluntarily left their homelands with the intention of becoming Americans, the Russian multinational state was built by conquest. Beginning with the absorption of the Muslim khanates of Kazan and Astrakhan in the mid–sixteenth century, Russia relentlessly expanded east, west, and south. Its acquisitions made it the largest state in the world.

The tsarist government did not pursue a consistent colonial policy, but by and large it did not interfere in the internal life of its subjugated peoples, some of whom, notably the Finns, it granted considerable powers of self-government. The most significant exception to the policy of benign neglect were the Poles who never reconciled themselves to the loss of independence: having failed to regain it by means of two rebellions, they only bided their time to throw off Russian domination. As a consequence, they were singled out for harsh treatment and Russification. Before 1917, the "national question" was only potentially a threat to the state's unity, as most of the ethnic minorities demanded nothing more than enhanced local autonomy. The consensus held that the question would solve itself as soon as tsarism gave way to a democratic regime.

The issue attracted the attention of Lenin who was forever seeking allies in his struggle for power. In common with the rest of the socialist community, he had no use for nationalism, Russian or any other, but unlike his rivals he saw the nationalists in the borderlands as potential partners in his struggle against tsarism and for this reason he was prepared to offer them—at least on paper—far-reaching concessions. In 1913 he formulated a national policy that granted every nationality inhabiting the Russian Empire the "right to self-determination" in the sense of the liberty to secede and form a sovereign state. Those that refused to avail themselves of this right, he expected to remain in the empire and assimilate: they were to receive no concessions that would institutionalize their ethnic consciousness. He was convinced that none of the minorities, the Poles included, would avail themselves of the power to secede from Russia because it was precluded by the growing economic interdependence of the country's diverse regions.

Events upset his plans. During the Revolution and the three-year struggle for power that ensued, most of the ethnic minorities proclaimed their independence and with the help, first of the Germans and then of the Allies, managed for a while to free themselves from Russia. But once the dust had settled only five—Finland, the three Baltic republics, and Poland—all on Russia's western borders, succeeded in making good their claim to sovereign status. The others were conquered, one by one, by the Red Army and incorporated into Soviet Russia with the West's tacit acquiescence.

Having violated his own "right to self-determination," Lenin made a volte-face and offered the minorities compensation intended to satisfy their thwarted national aspirations even though it inhibited their assimilation. It took the form of pseudo-federal status within a reconstructed Russian Empire supplemented with a limited amount of bureaucratic and cultural autonomy. The Union of Soviet Socialist Republics—the name "Russia" was dropped—formally constituted in 1924, consisted of a number of formally sovereign republics. Their sovereignty was formal because under the Soviet regime real power lay in the hands of the Russian Communist Party which, even after being renamed the Communist Party of the Soviet Union, was thoroughly dominated by Russians and assimilated non-Russians. The federal state apparatus merely executed orders issued to it by this party.

Along with this sham federalism, Moscow consented to a process labeled *korenizatsiia* or "indigenisation" by virtue of which executive power in the borderlands progressively passed into the hands of natives. Even this procedure, however, in practice turned out to be make-believe because behind every native in a position of authority stood a representative of the center, empowered to countermand his actions.

Cultural autonomy allowed the minorities the use of their native languages and a strictly controlled right to celebrate their

literature, art, and historic past. Anything that could be inter-
preted by the guardians of Russian hegemony as overstepping
permissible boundaries led to swift retaliation.

Notwithstanding the fact that throughout the history of the
Soviet Union the center of all power lay in Moscow, the pseudo-
federal structure of the state, *korenizatsiia*, and cultural autonomy,
restricted as they each were, inevitably promoted national self-
consciousness. Savage purges of minority intellectuals and officials for the crime of nationalism did not eradicate the sense of
ethnic pride and the striving for genuine statehood. If in 1917
only two of Russia's subject peoples—the Finns and the Poles—
desired independence, the quest for it now spread to every so-
called union republic.

Although the communist authorities insisted that their
country was a voluntary comity of free nationalities and not an
empire, at the first sign of disarray in Moscow the nationalities
began to clamor for the right to separate. The centrifugal forces
made themselves first felt in the Baltic region and the Caucasus,
but soon spread to the remaining borderlands. Georgia,
Lithuania, and Estonia declared independence in March 1991;
Latvia in May; Russia, Uzbekistan, and Moldova followed in
June; the Ukraine, the largest and most populous of the non-
Russian republics, along with Belarus declared themselves sovereign states in July 1991, a decision ratified on December 1 of that
year by over 90 percent of the Ukraine's population. Gorbachev's desperate efforts to preserve the Union by redrafting its
constitution availed nothing. It formally dissolved at the end of
1991 at the initiative of the president of Russia, Boris Yeltsin,

who had concluded that, in effect, it had ceased to exist. Thus, in the strict sense of the word, the collapse of the Soviet Union resulted from the dissolution of its empire brought about by the demands of its national minorities for independence.

———————————

If in the borderland regions dissent assumed the form of nationalist demands, inside Russia it expressed itself in demands for political and civil freedoms, especially the freedom of speech.

Lenin understood the importance of maintaining complete control over public opinion so well that the very first decree he issued upon assuming the chairmanship of the Council of People's Commissars called for the closure of all newspapers that refused to support the Bolshevik power seizure. He was too weak at the time to enforce this edict, but the following summer, in the course of the uprising of the Left SRs (Socialists-Revolutionaries), he finally succeeded in taking control of all printed media. With the creation in 1922 of *Glavlit*, the Main Administration for Literary Affairs and Publishing, all publications as well as the performing arts had to submit to preliminary censorship. In the 1920s a certain amount of freedom in the expression of independent opinions was still tolerated. This ended in the next decade when a deadly uniformity descended on Soviet intellectual and artistic life, all of it regulated from above to reinforce whatever policies the regime happened to pursue at a given moment.

The Soviet government did not care very much what its subjects really thought and felt as long as they conformed in word and deed. The result was that the population developed something akin to a split personality: outwardly it complied, inwardly it thought its own thoughts. This intellectual schizophrenia created in the Soviet Union a singularly oppressive atmosphere with people lying to the authorities which were quite aware they were being lied to and lied in turn.

After Stalin's death, and especially after Khrushchev's revelations of some of Stalin's crimes, voices of dissent began to be heard openly. Here and there, intrepid individuals expressed ideas that their more perceptive fellow citizens knew to be true but had kept to themselves. The majority tended to regard such dissenters as demented, an attitude the regime encouraged by confining some of them to psychiatric wards. All the same, the dissenters' message, reinforced by foreign broadcasts and contacts with visitors from abroad, had a destabilizing effect. With each passing year, Russians voiced more boldly what was on their minds, and the insistence on uniformity weakened appreciably.

The more intelligent among the Soviet leaders realized that the all-embracing censorship created a deceptive sense of universal support. Yet they did not dare to tamper with it. Yuri Andropov, the head of the KGB, and as such excellently informed of the true state of public opinion, confided to Markus Wolf, his East German counterpart, why censorship could not be lifted:

Too many groups have suffered under the repression in our country.... If we open up all the valves at once, and people start to express their grievances, there will be an avalanche and we will have no means of stopping it.

This was a realistic appraisal of the predicament in which the totalitarian regime found itself: theoretically omnipotent, it could do everything except allow its subjects to speak their mind from the fear of unleashing forces it would be unable to control.

Gorbachev's introduction of *glasnost* or "openness" was an act of desperation necessitated by the resistance of the *nomenklatura* to his program of reforms. The bureaucratic elite, fearful that these reforms would jeopardize its privileges, quietly sabotaged them. To overcome this opposition, Gorbachev appealed to public opinion. He apparently believed that the majority of Soviet citizens supported the communist regime and resented only its abuses. He was proved wrong: the outpouring of grievances showed that Andropov had more correctly appraised the situation and the dangers of opening up the media to dissenting views. With remarkable rapidity testing the limits of the allowable, Russians began to express publicly opinions that a short time ago would have landed them in the Gulag. The spell was broken.

Just what contribution the liberation of public opinion, at first cautious and then explosive, made to the downfall of the communist regime cannot be calculated, for we have no criteria by which to gauge the impact of such historic phenomena. But it can be said with confidence that without this breach of intellectual and psychological fetters it might never have occurred.

So much for the principal internal causes of communism's collapse. Of the external causes, the most decisive surely was the decision made by the United States in 1947–48 to meet head-on the challenge of Stalin's Cold War. The resolve with which the U.S. parried communist assaults during the next forty-five years, alike under Democratic and Republican administrations, is nothing short of astonishing, given the country's penchant for both impatience and isolationism. While it did not, by itself, bring down communism, without it communism might well have survived for many more decades.

Western Europe accommodated itself early to the Cold War and Soviet efforts at expansion in regions distant from the continent. It also readily acknowledged Eastern Europe as lying within the Soviet sphere of influence. A vivid example of this accommodation occurred in December 1981 during the imposition—on Soviet orders—of martial law in Poland, an action to which the U.S. responded with sanctions on both Poland and the USSR, but the German government declared to be an "internal" Polish affair. Essentially, NATO was a one-way street: it guaranteed U.S. intervention in the event the USSR attacked Western Europe but it did not commit Western Europe to assist the U.S. in its efforts to thwart communist expansion in other regions of the globe.

For one-third of the twentieth century—from the administration of Truman until the election of Reagan—U.S. policy toward the Soviet Union was essentially reactive. Its underlying assumption rested on the theory of containment which called on the U.S. to respond forcefully to any acts of Soviet aggression while, at the same time, collaborating with Moscow in every sphere where we had interests in common, be it arms control, scientific exchanges, or environmental protection. It seemed a sensible policy that enjoyed broad public support in the United States, if only because it carried the promise that close relations in the nonmilitary and nonpolitical spheres would, over time, bring the two countries closer together and reduce their mutual hostility.

The trouble with the containment principle was that it became outdated from the very moment of its formulation. Once the communists had taken over China, the most populous country in the world, containment turned into a hollow formula, inasmuch as it signified that communism had spilled beyond its original territory. And it kept on metastasizing: communist parties took control of North Korea and North Vietnam along with Cambodia, Cuba, Chile, Nicaragua, Ethiopia, and Afghanistan. Furthermore, in many countries of the Third World regimes came into being, which, while not avowedly communist, collaborated with the communists and for all practical purposes joined their bloc. Russia's rulers watched the spread of their influence around the globe with great satisfaction, for it promised in time to isolate the western camp and tip the world balance of power in their favor without resort to arms. To ensure their survival, they assisted communist and procommunist regimes with money, military equipment, and security personnel.

Successive U.S. administrations found it difficult to formulate a strategy to cope with these undesirable developments, sometimes acquiescing to communist aggression (e.g., in Hungary and Czechoslovakia), sometimes overreacting to it (e.g., in Cuba and Vietnam). But by the 1970s Washington settled on an eclectic policy of "detente" that assumed the Russians had the same interest in avoiding an armed conflict between the two countries as did the Americans. The result was an uneasy relationship of competition and collaboration that Moscow found very much to its taste.

Detente postulated that the Soviet regime was here to stay: it was stable and popular with its people and hence able to cope with whatever challenges to its authority emerged within its borders. This premise seemed borne out by history: did not the communists repel or neutralize every assault on their authority from the Russian civil war to the revolts in Eastern Europe? It seemed nothing short of quixotic to hope to undermine a government that enjoyed such a solid grip on its realm. This meant that, like it or not, one had to accept it such as it was and hope that time would soften its aggressive impulses.

This faith received legitimacy from the discipline of "Sovietology." Academic specialists on the Soviet Union agreed with a unanimity that should have aroused skepticism that we had no choice but to accommodate ourselves to the Soviet status quo because it was impervious to external pressures: any attempts to change it were not only counterproductive but exceedingly dangerous because, threatened from the outside, the Soviet government would react violently.

This consensus was challenged head-on by President Reagan. Reagan could claim little more than superficial knowledge of Russia and communist theory but he did possess a true statesman's intuition which told him that communism was not

Dear Reader:

Thank you for purchasing this Regnery book. Since 1947, we have published books on a wide variety of subjects. Often on the cutting edge of American and global affairs, our books are known for challenging the status quo. The book you have purchased is no exception.

If you would like to know more about our books, please fill out this postcard and drop it in the mail. Thank you.

Sincerely,

Alfred S. Regnery

Alfred S. Regnery
President & Publisher

**REGNERY
PUBLISHING, INC.**
Established 1947

Name ☐ Mr. ☐ Ms. ☐ Mrs. _____

Address _____

City _____ State _____ Zip _____

E-Mail _____

I received this card in the book titled _____

only evil but incapable of realization. Initially, upon assuming office, he believed, rather naively, that the leaders of the Soviet Union had the good of their people at heart and if they brought them nothing but misery it was because they had succumbed to a false doctrine. He thought that if he could sit down with them and explain why their country was so poor and backward, they would see the light and abandon Marxism-Leninism in favor of democracy and the market economy. In time, he learned this assumption to be wrong: the Soviet leadership and the elite that worked for it benefited from repression and poverty and hence had a vested interest in preserving both. This realization only intensified his anticommunism.

Reagan tacitly abandoned the containment policy that in any event had long been overcome by events. Rather than react to the Soviet Union's external behavior while acquiescing to its internal system, he went after the system itself on the premise that it was the true source of Soviet aggressiveness. This premise was articulated in National Security Decision Directive (NSDD) 75, which he signed in the winter 1982–83, a document that marked a fundamental shift in U.S. policy toward the Soviet Union by establishing a direct link between that regime's domestic and foreign policies. The critical passage occurred in the second paragraph of the executive summary. It declared that one of the principal tasks of U.S. foreign policy was

[t]o promote, within the narrow limits available to us, the process of change in the Soviet Union toward a

more pluralistic political and economic system in which the power of the privileged elite is gradually reduced. The US recognizes that Soviet aggressiveness has deep roots in the internal system, and that relations with the USSR should therefore take into account whether or not they help to strengthen the system and its capacity to engage in aggression.

This was a revolutionary concept, a shift from behaviorism which punished aggression and rewarded accommodation, to what postmodernists would call "essentialism."

The new course aroused furious opposition both in government and academic circles; in the daily press, the *Washington Times* was one of the few newspapers to endorse President Reagan's active policy. The State Department, which for two years had worked on its own policy paper that never managed to move beyond the clichés of detente, fought NSDD 75 tooth and nail, but secured only minor revisions. There was lukewarm support from the other departments of the executive: only Defense, headed by Caspar Weinberger, lined up behind it. Even the CIA reacted skeptically. Strobe Talbott, then a Soviet specialist for *Time* magazine and in the 1990s President Clinton's official in charge of Russian policy, wrote disdainfully in his *The Russians and Reagan*:

Speaking privately, [some] Administration officials, especially professional diplomats and intelligence analysts with long experience in Soviet affairs not only disavowed the notion that the United States could manipulate Soviet internal politics, but they expressed confidence that the Soviets recognized such theorizing for what it was: idiosyncratic, extremist, and very much confined to the fringes of government.

Both of Reagan's secretaries of state, Alexander Haig and George Shultz, convened private consultations of Soviet experts who, predictably, assured them it was "crazy" to think that the United States could influence internal developments in the USSR, let alone "bust" the USSR by means of economic warfare.

It is often said that Reagan intended to bankrupt the USSR by outspending it on the military. This, however, was not the policy: at any rate, during my two years on the NSC (1981–82) I never heard it articulated either publicly or privately. If during Reagan's presidency the United States spent a great deal on defense it was because the president genuinely worried that the Russians were striving for military superiority which he was determined to deny them.

The actual policy was to compel a shift in their budgetary priorities so that they would spend *less*, not more, on their armed forces. This was to be accomplished by significantly reducing their hard-currency earnings, especially those derived from energy exports. The strategy led to a nasty conflict between the U.S. and its allies in the spring of 1982 when President Reagan attempted to impose an embargo on the equipment for the Siberian gas pipeline that was expected by 1990 to earn Moscow $10 billion annually. The allies who were building pipeline compressors for the USSR under license from General Electric objected strenuously to U.S. demands that they cancel their contracts with Moscow on the grounds that such pressure represented an intolerable interference with their contractual commitments. In reality, it was they who violated contractual obligations because the licenses obtained by European manufacturers from GE, such as the French firm Alsthom-Atlantique, required them to abide by the terms of the Export Administration Act which President Reagan had invoked on grounds of national security. Reagan fought a losing battle on this issue but in the end he had his way because the 1980s witnessed a sharp drop in the price of petroleum, the Soviet Union's main export commodity.

Reagan also challenged communism with his rhetoric. On a number of occasions he publicly denounced it in a manner that the Russians thought ceased to be acceptable after they had acquired the capability to wage nuclear war. He irritated them not only with the content of his remarks but also their tone: neither angry nor apprehensive, but contemptuous, as in his 1981 speech at Notre Dame in which he announced that the free world would "transcend" communism. In 1988, during his visit to Moscow State University, as the *Washington Times* noted, he startled his audience by referring to Fredrich Hayek's observation that a cadre of bureaucrats cannot possibly replicate "the genius of the free market" under which millions of individuals exchange information and insight.

In sum, the United States, reluctantly and unreliably backed by its European allies, played a crucial role in deterring or at least slowing down Soviet expansion, frustrating its aspirations to military superiority, weakening its economy, and undermining its morale.

If the above analyses are correct, why is it that virtually no one foresaw the imminent collapse of communism in the Soviet Union? The consensus in and out of government was that the Soviet Union was an unalterable fact of life and that the West could do nothing about it except hope for its gradual mellowing.

When the author of this essay wrote in *Foreign Affairs* in the fall of 1984 that the USSR found itself in a "revolutionary situation," the "Sovietological" community thought the assertion so absurd that it did not even bother to react.

I believe that one of the main reasons why the profession missed all the clues pointing to a deep crisis of the communist regime was that its judgment was distorted by the fear of nuclear war. Intense study of the Soviet Union in the United States began only with Moscow's acquisition of nuclear weapons and accelerated with the launching, in 1957, of the Sputnik. In other words, Sovietology was born in the shadow of a potential Armageddon and as such it never acquired the detachment that is essential to all genuine scholarship and science: it was from the outset, and remained to the end, a prisoner of political concerns. To avoid nuclear war, it seemed imperative to maintain good, or at any rate, tolerable relations with the USSR. This, in turn, meant that one should stress positive developments in that country: criticism spelled confrontation. Faulty as the logic of such reasoning may have been, psychologically it was understandable. Such reasoning resulted in an intellectual ambience that made an objective study of the Soviet Union all but impossible: telling unpleasant truths about it became tantamount to "war mongering."

The other factor responsible for the failure of Sovietology had to do with the nature of modern social science. The immense prestige acquired by the natural sciences and their successes in both unlocking the mysteries of nature and harnessing them in the service of humanity influenced scholars engaged in the study of man and society to adopt their methods. Aristotle's *Politics* succumbed to Comte's *Sociology* with its emphasis on statistics and other mathematical tools.

One by-product of this evolution was the elimination of personal impressions: evidence based on them social science dismisses as "anecdotal" and, as such, unworthy of serious attention. Thus the CIA in the 1980s, relying on Soviet statistical data, declared the standard of living in the USSR to be 40 percent of the American. Because of its seemingly unimpeachable "scientific" nature, this assessment was widely accepted and drawn on to reinforce the policy of detente. However, anyone who spent an afternoon strolling, with open eyes, in the center of Moscow, the country's richest city, would in no time determine that its wealth was in no way comparable to that of the U.S.; if he extended his travels to the smaller provincial towns and even farther, to the rural districts, he would inescapably conclude that the country's living standards bore comparison only with the poorer countries of the Third World. Yet such judgments carried no weight because they were "anecdotal." The result was a very skewed picture of life in the USSR.

Another corollary of the application of the methods of the natural sciences to human affairs was the deliberate avoidance of moral judgments. The scientist, quite properly, approaches phenomena unemotionally. Thus a physician who examines a patient with a terminal illness does not adjust his diagnosis from sympathy for him and his family. But it has long ago been pointed out by such theorists as the Russians Peter Lavrov and

N. K. Mikhailovsky, that there is a fundamental difference between natural and human phenomena derived from the fact that, unlike the objects of the natural sciences, human beings have values and goals, for which reason social science cannot ignore moral factors, imponderable as they may be.

"Sovietologists" deliberately discounted values and goals in analyzing communist societies, in part because they were not quantifiable, and in part because they did not seem to matter to the social mechanism, the object of their study. But matter they did. A sensitive observer was bound to note the tension that pervaded communist societies from top to bottom from accumulated grievances that lacked outlets. Common sense dictated that regimes that insisted on 100 percent unanimity of public opinion or that punished with death citizens who tried to migrate, rested on very precarious foundations. Governments that were so much at odds with their population led, by their very nature, precarious existences, even if by the various means available to totalitarian regimes they could conceal this fact.

And finally there is the matter of history, or rather its neglect. Scientists have no use for the concept of "culture" because atoms and soils, plants and wild animals do not have "cultures" in the sense that human beings do, defined as the whole complex of values, rituals, and ways of doing things inherited from the past. These are deeply imbedded in the ethos of each society, from the small tribe to the nation-state. Social scientists, emulating their colleagues in the natural sciences, tend to ignore culture. They are uncomfortable with the notion that societies have imbedded in them cultures because it evokes "essentialism," the pernicious, to them, belief that things have "essences" rather than merely appearances susceptible to infinite interpretations.

In fact, knowledge of a country's culture is vital to the understanding of its behavior: for behavior is shaped not only by day-to-day experiences but also those which are bequeathed by previous generations. It is experience accumulated over centuries. Thus a person living in the West assumes that the money he deposits in a bank will retain its value and be available to him on demand. A Russian has no such expectations—for within living memory the ruble has lost virtually all its purchasing power and his bank deposits have been known to be frozen by government decree. A westerner treats a contract as a binding, legally enforceable obligation; a Russian regards it as a statement of intention between private parties that has no legal force. The commercial ethos teaches the westerner that every transaction must be of mutual benefit to the contracting parties, and for this reason he is amenable to compromises. The Russian, lacking this tradition, views each transaction as a zero-sum game and treats compromise as either surrender or opportunism.

One could lengthen such a list to explain how the past has conditioned Russians to react differently from westerners to similar situations. Such knowledge is surely necessary if one is to anticipate Russian behavior.

A telling example is the approach to nuclear weapons. Americans, acting on the rational premise that victory in war makes sense only if the gains are greater than the losses, and attaching the highest value to human lives, developed a nuclear strategy known as Mutual Assured Destruction (MAD). It assumed that because the casualties from a nuclear exchange would be so staggering that no sane party would resort to it unless it itself faced obliteration, nuclear weapons could serve only one purpose, namely deterrence. From this it followed that once a country had built up its arsenal of offensive weapons to the point where any attacker would face annihilation in a retaliatory strike, war became senseless and hence ceased to be an option.

But this logic had no appeal to the mind of the Russian military. To them, war was war and its object was victory: this principle was unaffected by the nature of the weapons employed. Such was the doctrine formulated by Marshal V. D. Sokolovskii in his authoritative manual, *Military Strategy*. In his view, while nuclear war ought to be avoided if at all possible, victory in it was attainable by a combination of superiority in offensive weapons and defensive measures. Losses in human lives, while regrettable, could be absorbed. The most blunt expression of this point of view was articulated by Mao Tse-tung:

> If worst came to the worst and half of mankind died, the other half would remain while imperialism would be razed to the ground and the whole world would become socialist; in a number of years there would be 2,700 million people again and definitely more.

We now know from the memoirs of Nikita Khrushchev's son that in 1961 Fidel Castro urged Moscow to launch a preemptive nuclear strike against the United States which, even though it would destroy Cuba, would lead to the worldwide triumph of communism.

Such a manner of thinking was so alien to American analysts that they chose to ignore it, insisting that the communists, too, adhered to the MAD doctrine as the only rational strategy. Moscow's relentless buildup of offensive weapons in the 1970s, after it had attained parity with the United States, in such stark contradiction to the principles of MAD, was rationalized in various ways but not taken as evidence that the Russians had a war-fighting and war-winning strategy, as confirmed by Soviet military experts after the breakup of the USSR.

Winston Churchill is quoted as saying that Americans usually get things right but only after exhausting all the other possibilities. Indeed, in the momentous confrontation with Soviet power, we have committed many mistakes, swinging wildly from the Red Scare of the 1920s, to the romantic illusions of the 1930s which reached their climax during World War II, back to McCarthy's anticommunist hysteria, then again to the mirages of detente and "convergence." But in the end, a combination of resolve and patience accomplished their objective: the Soviet Union and its client states dissolved and they did so without a shot being fired between the principal antagonists in the struggle.

If there are any lessons to be drawn from this historic experience, they may be summarized as follows: (1) that utopian thinking inevitably leads to the worst excesses and the very opposite of its intentions, and (2) that in dealing with this phenomenon, it is necessary to view it on its own terms and not impose on it values borrowed from other cultures. This knowledge, backed by self-confidence and determination, is most likely to carry the day.

A Nation
Turning
in a New
Direction

MIDGE DECTER

Midge Decter

Midge Decter, a New York writer and editor noted for her contribution to magazines such as *Commentary* and *Harpers*, is the author of four books, including *Liberal Parents, Radical Children*. She sits on The Heritage Foundation's board of directors and was a fellow at the Institute on Religion and Public Life.

s the twentieth century drew to a close, Americans were in an odd condition. Naturally, there was much talk about, and much anticipation of, the new millennium: as if the process of shifting into a new century—as distinct from moving merely into a new year—would vouchsafe some kind of special and unprecedented turning in the order of things. (In the event, of course, September 11, 2001, would bring a seismic shift in both the country's life and the public temper, but far from the one speculated about in 1999.) Whether this Year 2000-turning would prove to be genuinely one of the spirit or merely some unnamable kind of shift of temporal circumstance was a question pretty much left hanging in the air. But that something large would have happened as the calendar moved to New Year's Day 2000 millions of people seemed to be in no doubt. And New Year's Eve 2000 took on a certain added air of celebratory frenzy. The country had just been through strange times with a young, politically clever, and very badly behaved president who would perforce be leaving office in 2001. This president, who

could fairly be called the Man of the Nineties, had by turns been embraced, reviled, and reembraced by his own liberal constituents. They had for a brief moment permitted themselves to display some disgust with his private conduct, but quickly recovered themselves in the face of the conservative enemy who appeared to be gathering strength just outside the gates of the kingdom.

There was, after all, no room, the liberals properly understood, for a weakening of the ranks. Back in 1994 they had been frightened by what appeared to be an explosion of conservative political strength, but as he would on more than one occasion, their president would outwit the conservatives at several critical junctures, more than once by beating them—or at least appearing to beat them—at their own game. Thus the country's conservatives—at first overconfident and then put off course—would not actually consolidate their winnings and genuinely take over the government. That, in fact, they would not do until the new millennium—and even then only by a hair.

Needless to say, then, any fantasy that the year 2000 would bring with it some large event or awakening would quickly be obscured in the midst of all the old familiar strivings and enmities. As it happens, electoral politics has always been the poorest indicator of the cultural and spiritual condition of the country. Naturally there is almost always some connection between how people feel in their everyday lives and how they vote, but that connection is almost always a fairly tenuous, or at least a very complicated, one. For people must always be left to vote on the choice that is put before them, and that choice is itself usually dependent on many circumstances that have little or nothing to do with their actual feelings. Rarely do the two come together, as they did for so many millions of people, for instance, in the case of the election of Ronald Reagan. And in that case, it was not Reagan's views on taxation, say, or indeed any other specifics of his policy, that moved vast constituencies in the country to vote for him. Rather, it was his expressed determination that the United States be restored to the conduct, and the faith, of a great nation that released a huge wave of popular gratitude—particularly coming off the joint depression of the Vietnam fiasco and the charge of the ultimately witless Mr. Carter in the late 1970s that the country's "malaise" had been the people's rather than his own.

As president, Reagan had done many things (and had left many others undone), but what mattered most was that he told ordinary Americans what they had been longing, unrequited, to hear, and he helped them to believe what they had been longing, without encouragement, to believe: that the United States was good and could and would be better, and that the country's enemies would not prevail. This, of course, earned him a reputation among the cognoscenti for being simpleminded—a charge that was completely ignored by ordinary Americans.

What was missing from the presidency of Reagan's successor—and what cost him reelection—was precisely this: he had no confirming message. In particular, having put on a great light-and-heat show over Iraq, he left untouched the man he had earlier so passionately declared to be an evil aggressor on the grounds that the American-led coalition would be unwilling to pay the cost of final victory. He did not say "malaise," but critics charged that his policy did. And once again the national spirit sank, and was made ready to be outwitted by the young unprincipled "new" liberal (and his most determinedly old-style liberal wife) who was carried into the presidency in 1992.

In preparing the first campaign of this "Man of the Nineties," his chief strategist James Carville had memorably defined what it was that would in the end be responsible for his election success: "It's the economy, stupid." But in fact, the idea that people vote their pocketbooks is almost always wrong: the economy, too, is usually subsumed under issues of the spirit, and this was never more the case than in 1992. In the nineties, as we know, and no thanks either to the new president or his so clever adviser, money would prove to be both plentiful and easily come by. Through their savings and investments large numbers of middle-class people found themselves to be the possessors of more wealth than they might earlier have dreamed of. And for the young, especially, there were previously unimaginable possibilities. The Soviet Union had collapsed. Throughout Central Europe there were peoples beginning to test out the possibilities, along with the anxieties, of self-government. So there was a new world, and the United States was sitting atop it.

Moreover, between Wall Street and that whole congeries of industries stemming from the powers of the microchip, fortunes were being made, occasionally lost, remade, and remade again—

and often those who made them were barely more than kids. In any case, large numbers of people experienced an increase of some dimension, from small to truly palpable, in their standard of living. They traveled, they vacationed, they recreated, they saw the great wide world, and they planned as never before for how to advantage their children. All of this might have seemed to a casual observer from elsewhere to bespeak a great moment of national contentment. But that was far, very far, from being so. For the newly hopeful international situation had released the country to turn inward to a whole new extent, and the decade would thus be given over very largely to old, long unsettled, and now newly exfoliated quarrels over who was to determine the nature and quality of American society. In short, the country had for some time been culturally and spiritually split, and the new turn inward had left people going head to head perhaps even more intently than ever before over issues as deep as those of life and death in areas where there seemed to be no hope of reconciliation.

The issues tearing at the country in the nineties were precisely those that had sunk the deepest into people's immediate, everyday lives: issues of life and death, of how to define an acceptable common culture, of how to raise and to educate the children. If one had to give relative weight to these issues—an admittedly rather difficult task—probably the problem of abortion would come first: for abortion, both the issue and the act, brings in its train many agitated questions that go far beyond merely that of unwanted pregnancy, questions concerning attitudes toward sex, marriage, children, and ultimately life itself.

Now, agitation over abortion was certainly not new to the nineties: it had been roiling near the surface of politics, particularly local politics, since the 1950s, when state legislature after state legislature was being beset annually by delegations vociferously demanding that abortion be legalized, delegations made up in about equal parts of independently activist women and representatives of the movement called Planned Parenthood. Not surprisingly, by the late 1960s, many of these delegations had been enlarged, or taken over, by representatives of the recently declared feminist revolution, who began here and there to achieve their goal. One of the features of this new campaign—it would prove to be more successful with the legislators and far more consequential for the future—was that whereas Planned Parenthood had barely concealed its true focus, which was to reduce the birthrate of the indigent, particularly among the blacks, the feminists were demanding the right to unconditioned and unfettered abortion for *themselves*—and ultimately for their young daughters. In short, they were, and promised to remain, concerned voters.

Then had come 1973, and the Supreme Court decision in the case of *Roe v. Wade*, which legitimated abortion in the first trimester of pregnancy—a period of time that would come to be greatly lengthened down through the years. In any case, now the issue had ostensibly been taken out of mere politics and had been given the sanction of nothing less than the Constitution of the United States, of which it had so famously been seen by Justice Blackmun as a "penumbra" derived from an "emanation." This might have been thought to settle the problem, and in fact legal abortion clinics were opened and grew busy throughout the land. But the question of abortion, as anyone politically sensitive might have known, would not, and could not, be settled, even by Supreme Court fiat, because there remained large sectors of the American public who continued to regard abortion as murder, both a sin and a crime, and they continued to agitate and demonstrate against it in every way they knew how (including on occasion, alas, outright bloodshed). Another reason the issue of abortion could not be definitively settled was that many enlightened young feminists, those in whose name much of the fight to legalize abortion had been waged, reached the age of desire to become mothers and began to discover that they felt a certain confusion on the issue. They would not join the party of the Right-to-Lifers, but they could no longer be relied on to be in the forefront of the proabortion campaign, either.

Moreover, something new and dangerous to their advocacy was the fact that as members of the proabortion party, they were now being required to expose the absolute unconditionality of their commitment, through the newly publicized problem of late-term abortions. Late-term abortions are those performed on fully grown, late- or even full-term viable babies who are usually disposed of by crushing their heads as they are pulled through the birth canal. Those who had maintained that abortion was not

murder were now required to make their argument in the face of a practice whose murderousness required a good deal of fancy intellectual footwork to deny. All this kept the issue not only roiling in the American streets but on the front burner of politics into the nineties.

Somewhat separate, but not unrelated, issues were those raised around the same time by the ongoing research into human genes: questions of whether or how to make use of left-over fetal material produced by the abortionists or by normal stillbirths and what to do with all the fertilized ova left over from the efforts, successful or unsuccessful, at in vitro fertilization. This latter technology had produced miracles for many seemingly infertile couples—the polar opposite, you might say, of abortion—but yet it had also become one not free of deeper, and sometimes truly darker, issues for humans to contemplate. Most people, it seems fair to say, had not even dreamed of the power that, as they were to discover in the nineties, had been put into the hands of scientists. And with such power, there came a number of terrible human issues that they would soon, without adequate spiritual means, be forced to contemplate.

There was the movement for the legalization of assisted suicide—a movement, after all, that sought to argue questions belonging somewhere on the continuum from new life to death. This movement had suffered a blow with the arrest of one of its two leading and most colorful advocates, Dr. Jack Kevorkian (the other being Derek Humphrey). Only in the state of Oregon would it be given formal (but still continuously challenged) legality. But the issue of assisted suicide, agitated in itself, further roused a question that would not be so easily settled, as many fine and highly civilized minds felt obligated to take up the agonizing problem of whether it is more compassionate to continue treating the terminally ill, merely to keep them alive, or more loving and compassionate merely to ease their pain as much as possible and let them die.

Religions had in the past addressed this question, but now it confronted the world in the elaborate trappings of a science that had already proved itself capable of bringing back to ordinary life those who could earlier not have been saved. Mere mortals had thus been given sometimes the illusion, sometimes the reality, of a new power over life and death. How were they then to think and act? And how could the issues posed by abortion not have shadowed this discussion? Moreover into the air at about the same time had come the possibility of human cloning—if not immediately, then at some time in the future. Should we then surgically (or medicinally) dispose of real babies while at the same time we sanction the creation of artificial ones? And to be put to what purpose? These are questions that probably cause most ordinary mortals to wish to shut off their minds, and yet there they are, and as the nineties taught us, from now on will not easily go away.

Another issue, seemingly unrelated to abortion, but not at all unrelated to the kind of mechanized, and hence brutalized, advocacy that found its ultimate expression in late-term abortions, had been the country's enlightened liberal thinking on the issue of the blacks. Like abortion, this is an issue that has long been debated in the United States, and while it has a great deal more day-to-day complexity than abortion, it similarly seems to defy any possible adjudication either of attitudes or of policies. Once the determination had been reached to requite America's blacks for the bitter injustices they had endured both before and after their emancipation from slavery—a process that moved slowly through the body politic from, say, the early 1950s to the Civil Rights Act of 1965—there ensued a debate about the country's obligation to the blacks and the blacks' obligation to themselves that raged (and "raged" is the word) with a kind of steady ferocity that had not abated by the nineties.

Essentially, however, this debate was one that raged not so much between blacks and whites as between liberals and conservatives, with millions of people who were committed to neither one side of the argument nor the other being moved this way and that by passing circumstance. The argument, of course, had first, and fatefully, centered on the schools, it having been the decision of the civil rights movement that the schools should be their major target and that the only fair and decent education for black kids was to be had in racially integrated classrooms, and to push for that first. This demand resulted in something that neither black nor nonblack parents wanted, namely, the crossbusing of children away from their neighborhood schools to ostensibly integrated classrooms in schools some distance away. The policy failed, as anyone less ideologically blindered than people out to do good as they saw it come what may might have predicted: children who had the advantage of a choice, either in private schools or in suburbs, simply left the public schools, and those who had no choice but to remain not only often found themselves in largely, or even completely, segregated classrooms, but they might as easily as not be pulled away from better neighborhood schools and sent off to worse ones far away (as happened under court enforcement in Boston).

What had followed—as, you might say, the night the day—was the policy known as affirmative action, represented early on as merely a means of seeking out qualified and unjustly disadvantaged blacks and helping them to their just share of such of the world's goods as elite college placements. Like the opponents of enforced public school integration, the opponents of affirmative action were labeled as selfish and racially hostile. And the policy swept like wildfire, not only through the processes of college admissions but, by means of a long-denied practice of race-norming, in grading as well—and subsequent to graduation, in hiring.

Another result of the contest to "solve" the racial discrimination problems created earlier by compounding them with more racial discrimination on the other side was the impulse among large numbers of black college students, who found themselves in schools for which they were not qualified, to band together and segregate themselves from their fellows, in classrooms devoted to a travesty called "black studies" as well as in their living quarters and places of recreation. Thus, long advertised as a boon to disadvantaged blacks, affirmative action in practice had, in all too many cases, exactly the opposite effect on its intended beneficiaries, leaving them, whatever their level of achievement, with the stigma of lack of qualification. All of this was, of course, thoroughly in train long before the century's final decade, and yet it once again became, or perhaps the word is remained, at the center of an almost unreconcilable cultural divide—further compounded by the evidence of what was happening to vast numbers of young blacks, particularly young black males, left beyond the pale of ordinary life. These males, raised without fathers by often either lost or overwhelmed mothers, and failed by elementary school systems that had long been turned away from anything remotely resembling their once-upon-a-time pedagogic ambition, were basically left to roam the streets and there create for themselves a facsimile society based on the ethos of the gangs—whose highest social status was conferred on those toughened by prison.

The debate continued to rage over the question of what to do about these young men and the ongoing, casual, murderous violence usually predicted by their mere presence on the scene—along with the much-agitated issue of how to deal with all the illegitimate, government-supported babies they cheerfully fathered on their teenage female neighbors and then abandoned. Essentially this debate, once carried on in burning sorrow, had by the nineties boiled down to the old liberal idea that what they needed was rehabilitation and jobs (and it would be the government's ultimate responsibility to provide them) against a rather newer and firm, though despondent, conservative idea that society for its own protection seemed to have no other recourse than to incarcerate them and keep on doing so until they simply grew too old for their former life on the streets.

Though the national conversation about what to do with, or about, these young men had also been going on since the sixties, few events served as a more vivid reminder of the issue than the black-on-white, black-on-Korean, and ultimately black-on-black riot in South Central Los Angeles from April 29 to May 3, 1992. The particular circumstance of this riot has receded into the mists of memory: how a black man named Rodney King, a frequent tangler with the law, was stopped by the police for drunk driving, violently resisted arrest, and was thereupon sorely chastised by the police. This scene having been caught on the videocamera of a nearby onlooker and subsequently broadcast over and over across the land, the policemen involved were soon thereafter indicted and tried. Upon their having been found not guilty by a jury of their peers, almost immediately all hell broke loose and stayed that way for days, featuring guns, rocks, fires, looting, and general murderous mayhem. The damage wreaked during those four and a half days was said to have totaled anywhere from $750 million to one billion dollars.

The "enlightened" press, certain members of the activist-liberal bar, psychologists, social workers, and a sprinkling of all-weather-compassionate public figures hastened to explain what had happened in the terms customary to their discourse (racism-cum-unemployment-cum-poverty-cum-police brutality-cum-summertime, etc.), but this time everyone in the land had been enabled to watch in full and intimate detail just what had gone on at the riot's ground zero, and it had been pure joyful ugliness followed by the intoxication of mass looting.

The Los Angeles riot of 1992, then, seems to have become for many a kind of watershed in the problems of the criminality of America's young male ghetto denizens, with less immediate emphasis on the social etiology of their condition and a good deal more on the question of how society is to defend itself against them. This is an issue that continues to produce some debates, but also many arrests for infractions both large and small, and many new jails—along with much political, and even journalistic, celebration of a newly heightened safety in the American streets. It seems no coincidence that the following year brought with it the New York City mayoralty of Rudolph Giuliani and his celebrated intolerance for the minor infractions of public order that lead inevitably to the major ones.

Meanwhile, here and there in major cities throughout the country something had been going on largely out of sight as well as out of mind of the general public—something that would only be brought to wider public attention by the newly elected George Bush in the new decade to come: the growth of a variety of programs, most of them church-related and all of them faith-based, for turning around the lives of the inner-city black children who were being so badly failed by the ministrations of both an allegedly benign social service system and an allegedly tough criminal justice system. These programs, run from within their own community and usually (though not always) by clergymen, were doing precisely what, after its first heroic campaign to overcome Jim Crow, the civil rights movement had unhappily been distracted from doing for them: namely, teaching them how to rescue themselves. Little by little these largely church-based efforts—need it be said that they were in constant need of funds and other kinds of support that were not as forthcoming as they needed to be?—were being brought more and more to the attention of a rather small but deeply concerned and encouraged public as well as, fatefully, to the attention of the man who would be elected president in 2000 and who would attempt to create the means for offering them government largesse. And one of the few media organs bringing this information to the public was the *Washington Times*, which had for years been regularly spotlighting such small, faith-inspired social service groups.

But to return to the dominant institutionalized forms of public beneficence to the needy, the country's school systems also came to adopt the idea that Hispanic children, in the beginning the offspring of new immigrants and hence unpracticed in English, should be taught for some years in their native language. This was advertised as a compassionate, and also a correct, pedagogic measure, and before anyone, especially any Hispanic parent, had been enabled to debate the issue, the system was put in place. Which meant purely and simply that some untold number of Hispanic children would be forced into a constant uphill battle to learn anything—deprived of the benefit of what had once been an entirely earnest and unselfconscious glory of American public education, namely, its adoption of the role of making young citizens of the immigrant children given into its care. By the nineties, the opposition to this putatively compassionate "educational" experiment had become not only enormous (that it had been for a long time) but highly voluble, including on the part of Hispanic parents who had at last begun to find their voice. Finally, against the collective will of the whole educational apparatus that had grown up around this program, in 1998, bilingual education was struck down by ballot in the state of California, thanks to the energy and determination of a man named Ron Unz and those of his supporters; and if in California, perhaps the rest of the nation will not lag too far behind.

If the problems connected with educating the immigrant poor and racially disadvantaged may have been what originally appeared to set off a crisis in American public education, something else was continuing to make it very nearly intractable. And that was something that can only be called the country's careless attitude toward itself. Perhaps such carelessness might overtake any country that was as vast, rich, powerful—and as safely situated—as the United States; but perhaps, too, there is a particularly American problem that lies in the heart of the country's political culture: a kind of taking for granted, an acquisition of the country's social and economic and political goods on what is taken to be an unending, and never to be collected from, line of credit, the sense that no amount of battering from outside or in can really shake or damage the foundations, that, in short, the country can withstand any amount of punishment or lack of care with its institutions.

This is a feeling given to people when they are experiencing great benefit, and do not really imagine that they might cease one day to do so. And nowhere has it been more on display in recent years than in the country's educational establishments, primary, secondary, or higher.

Indeed, it would seem that to ignore or attack the country's institutions, and the ways of life and sensibilities of its ordinary citizens, has become the highest calling of American education. There are many more important, but no more vivid, illustrations of this than the "celebration" of the five-hundredth anniversary of the landing of Christopher Columbus in the New World in

1492. The anniversary in 1992, having been prepared for by numerous public educational agencies (including the redoubtable Smithsonian Institution) was converted, especially for the benefit of the country's schoolchildren, into an occasion of deep and outright mourning: Columbus's discovery, it seemed fitting for the authorities to teach, had led to nothing more than the dispossession, immiseration, and outright slaughter of native peoples. The children were thus given the choice of reviling their own presence on American soil or signing on with the alien invaders. Some protests were issued from among the ranks of the country's conservatives, but the event passed too quickly for the protesters to have had much effect. Happily, however, such bizarre examples of political correctness that came to be embodied in the phenomenon known as multicultural education were frequently reported and commented upon by the *Washington Times*.

In any case, there was too much else to worry about. For by all the standard measures of achievement in such basic skills as reading and math, not to mention such "frills" as the history of their country, it was now undeniable to all but the most blindered educators that any special problems of the black community aside, American public school children were shockingly lacking, both by comparison with American children of the past and by comparison with children from other countries. This, too, was hardly a new issue for the nineties, but it was taking on a new urgency with the evidence of a growing rebellion among the public.

For everywhere voices were beginning to be raised with various demands: to overhaul the country's system of public education through competition with private or parochial schools, or by taking it away from the presently constituted educational bureaucracy altogether and placing it in some way into the hands of parents and/or concerned citizens. And there were those, few but growing in number, who advocated simply destroying it and starting over in some completely new way. As much as President Bush coveted the appellation the "education president," it was the *Washington Times* that truly deserved the moniker, "the education newspaper," for it devoted endless column inches to covering America's schools, and the radical need for radical reform, at every level. When most of the major media seemed to shrink from giving editorial space or air time to advocates of free-market-oriented education reforms, the *Times* went ahead full bore in that vein. And in the midst of all this discussion, the idea of school vouchers, which would enable children to take either their share of the state's education money, or the bounty from some kind of private philanthropy, and carry it with them into any school of their choosing, had begun here and there to move from the stage of experimental thinking into the realm of reality.

Another idea on the boards that was being carried out experimentally here and there, either through private philanthropy or under the aegis of an occasional public school system, was that of the charter school, a school that would be independently run by a principal and his or her chosen teachers in accordance with his independently arrived at cultural outlook and principles of ped-agogy. And there has been a growing, though statistically not yet significant, number of parents who have undertaken to teach their children at home. Many of these last, to be sure, are seri-ously believing Christians who have rebelled against the moral and religious aridity of the schools (if not their open and pre-scribed hostility to all things religious); but since it appears that children educated at home achieve a great deal more in far less time than others, the practice may grow.

Fatefully for American education, all of these ideas—not all of them, to be sure, without serious problems of their own—were heartily opposed by the teachers' unions, who felt that their own future welfare was tied up with the public school system as it was, that is, requiring only more money: money to clean up the school buildings, to expand them, to engage more teachers in order to reduce class size, to pay them better, to make recruit-ment easier, and so on. Since the teachers' unions are large and politically powerful organizations, they have managed, to growing public antipathy—for after all, there is no necessary reason in logic for teachers to have plighted their troth to a clearly failing institution—to remain an impediment to any serious plans for improving the schools. The debate over this issue raged through the nineties and promises to continue at least through the presidency of George W. Bush, as he has gone far beyond his father in his engagement with the school problem, a problem with which he claims having had some real success as governor of Texas.

Those who do not foresee destroying the public school system in order to save it have proposed such measures as the imposition of national standards to be determined by uniform national testing; others have said that it is the teachers who need periodic testing. Those ordinary citizens, possibly fewer in number than they used to be, who sided with the liberals and the teachers' representatives in saying that what the schools need is more and more money, appeared on the whole to remain content, at least with the schools their own children attended. And as for the blacks, with whom some part of this problem had started, or through whom at least it had at first been exposed, by

the time the nineties rolled around it was at last being recognized that a significant number had taken themselves out of the central cities and the poverty bespoken there, had quietly moved well into the middle class, and into the suburbs. There they will almost certainly, sooner or later, be joining with their nonblack fellow suburbanites in agonizing over the schools that had played such a large part in their moving beyond the cities.

Still, one of the consequences of this development, as we have seen, is that it has helped in its own way to intensify some of the problems of the inner cities by leaving them so largely at the mercy of the gangs of those young men among whom neither the threat nor the reality of law enforcement comes attended with any fear. (Whether or not the very hopeful faith-based programs mentioned above will acquire sufficient salience to overmaster this problem remains to be seen; at any rate, it is given in the very nature of such efforts that they must take time, working, as the title of an important book by the black economist Glenn Loury has it, "one by one from the inside out.") At least so far, as was made clear in the aftermath of the Los Angeles riot, a term in prison has for too many become the ultimate entitlement to the estate of manhood. Moreover, as the nineties wore on, the increasing possibility that their women, the mothers of their children, would be forced off the government dole and into some kind of gainful employment seemed to have had no impact on their behavior. (What impact the requirement that they go to work, to the extent that it is truly enforced, will have on the women who were once the recipients of welfare cannot yet be judged. But one thing, scanted by all sides to the debate about the benefits versus the cruelty of welfare reform that roiled the nineties, seems certain in at least the early years following the nineties: the marriage of the mothers to the fathers of their babies in this community will if anything become even less likely.)

In a sense, to speak of the tribulations of the schools is to place the cart before the horse. For though they are in a sense institutions heavily weighed down by years of overgovernment, encrusted with bureaucracy, and spooked with educational superstitions, they are also highly responsive reactors to the tides of the culture outside. If their theories of pedagogy remain largely in thrall to what were the advanced intellectual, particularly the psychological, fashions of the 1930s, what they see fit to teach is very much in thrall to the parade passing just outside their windows. And in that respect, the atmosphere of the nineties seemed from a certain point of view to be the most careless of all.

Now, as it happened, the march of Black Power followed by that of Women's Liberation had some time earlier begun to slow to a halt—or perhaps it should be said, had become so tightly integrated into the culture as to be almost no longer visible. To be sure, debate about such issues as racial and/or ethnic preferences continued (and would continue into the twenty-first century) to roil the conservative community—as did passionate countercultural assertions of the necessity of such now-devalued institutions as marriage and family. But among the major institutions of cultural dissemination—the schools, of course, and beyond them the so-called "elite" press, the arts, the high-status universities, and to a not inconsiderable extent even certain agencies of federal, state, and local government—had fully surrendered to the pressure exerted by militant blacks and women.

To be sure, for many years there had been well-organized and lively opposition to the women's movement, all of it from within the conservative community—the names of Phyllis Schlafly and Beverly LaHaye come most immediately to mind. Indeed, to the shock of the National Organization of Women, this opposition had succeeded in defeating the Equal Rights Amendment to the Constitution. But the day-to-day work of sexual preference, the enlargement, spread, and criminalization of the idea of "sexual harassment," and such practices as sexual integration of the military academies and armed forces had nevertheless gone on apace. By the mid-nineties, however, something new had entered upon the scene of women's politics, namely, the organizing into an opposition to the movement of a group of young women who were the counterparts of the very young women it had been the movement's real purpose to speak for: lawyers, government officials, journalists, scientists, academics, doctors, and so on, trained career women who felt demeaned by the movement's claims on their behalf and who set out, not like Phyllis Schlafly to create a new body of voters, but to unleash a new body of counterarguments against the movement's claims. In so doing, they have managed to triangulate a so far relatively modest membership into a growing and unignorable source of power. By the end of the century, the most successfully organized group of this kind was the Washington-based Independent Women's Forum. And the group's success so far will very likely encourage the creation of others around the country focused on local issues. Through all this hubbub, the *Washington Times* supported the feminist backlash by running articles about the extremist excesses of the radical feminists and the measured deliberations of the IWF and other dissidents.

One cultural parade that was left to make its full mark in the nineties, however, was that of the so-called "gay" liberation movement. If certain state legislatures remained resistant to the demand of this movement for the right of homosexual couples to legal marriage—with all that such a measure would suggest not only of economic entitlements for gay "spouses" but of full social acceptance of the nature of homosexual life and behavior—the elite culture was offering its complete approval and encouragement. In books, movies, plays, magazines, operas, major news media, along with the profession of psychiatry and the administrations of many colleges and universities, homosexuality was coming at one and the same time to be granted full equality and special victim status. Moreover, what might in another time have been considered something of a puzzle was the effect on the high estate of male homosexual relations of the fact that they had only recently been found to come attended with a devastating disease, called Acquired Immune Deficiency Syndrome. AIDS, it was discovered, is a disease that, in the West at least, attends basically two kinds of behavior: repeated careless male sexual promiscuity and unclean intravenous drug injection. (For a while, the homosexual-rights movement, perhaps fearing opprobrium, attempted to claim that everyone was at risk, but this claim did not survive the passage of time.)

Before medical science had been able to come up with an (exorbitantly expensive) medication that blocks the disease from moving beyond a preliminary stage, untold numbers of homosexuals were sentenced to a painful death. Nor from time to time would numbers among them be persuaded to change their behavior so as to avoid the disease. But the onset and spread of AIDS only seemed to provide the homosexual community with an added measure of public sympathy and cultural approval. Perhaps the most confirming symbol of this approval, though to be sure not the deepest going, was the moment at which the movie star Tom Hanks stood up before a coast-to-coast audience, and, accepting an academy award for his movie performance of a man stricken with AIDS, wept and declared he was accepting the award "for all those angels in heaven"—a gesture that appeared to earn him widespread admiration and empathy. Nor, predictably, would the American public education system be spared the fallout from this liberation movement, as it had not been from the others. In a number of places homosexual activists were invited to participate in devising new sex-education curricula whose underlying purpose was to teach the children—beginning in the first grade—about the ways and means of homosexual mating so they should from the very first learn to be tolerant, and, more than tolerant, accepting. It is hard to gauge how effective this effort has really been, since many teachers simply shelved the curricula as being too long and complicated for their own comfort. But the point is, the educators and publishers had enthusiastically embraced these programs.

It is naturally not easy to pinpoint from whence comes the refusal, or inability, of a society—even in its public institutions—to protect its youngest children from the kind of unasked-for and chillingly premature introduction to the details of sexual relations that provided so easy an opening to the ideologues of "gay" sex. This inability has many sources, but perhaps the most important of these has been the abdication of the educated middle class from its indispensable role of holding, and embodying the values of, that great solid ground on which this society has for so long remained stable. The process of weakening American self-confidence had, to be sure, been going on in many different areas of the life of this society since (if it is possible to date such things) the early 1960s. But perhaps because the great and widespread wealth of the nineties had made life so easy for so many, or perhaps just because the undermining from the top of the culture down through its ordinary everyday manners and habits had been going on so long, the final decade of the century witnessed what seemed to many to be the ultimate collapse of public standards: standards of social behavior, of sexual decency, and perhaps, above all, of intellectual and artistic probity.

For without the resistance of that once solid middle, clinging to what it knows to be both true and valuable, there was now virtually nothing, neither government nor private establishment nor community of taste, to resist the wild cyclonic winds of fashion. Take the case of the visual arts, which down through the years had benefited so much from the necessity to carry on against the suspicion and resistance of the day-to-day public (artists crying in rage against this resistance and at the same time being sharpened and deepened by it). These artists were now liberated to claim wide swaths of new territory for their estate.

Untold numbers of objects and combinations of objects from piles of bricks to motorcycles to neon-light installations to reclaimed discarded plumbing fixtures now found their places of honor in the museums whose special pride is to keep the public acquainted with the ever renewing new; and among these "works" equally newly trained critics and appreciators solemnly made their way: nothing offends, nothing displeases. A crucifix in a jar of urine became the occasion for a great national debate about artistic freedom versus censorship, the artistic community and its bureaucrats firing smoking charges of ignorance and backwardness across the bows of those who took religious, not to speak of esthetic, offense at this display. The same fate awaited those only somewhat later who dared to take umbrage at a certain painting of the Virgin splattered with, among other things, elephant dung—not to mention an exhibition of photographs by a homosexual artist named Robert Mapplethorpe who "beautifully" and lovingly photographed himself with a bullwhip in his anus or a man urinating into another man's mouth. It was simply no longer possible to raise issues of taste or public sensibility—

let alone that of artistic standards—even in connection with tax-payer-funded institutions—when the terms "art" and "artistic freedom" were invoked. And the importance of government funding in all this cannot be scanted.

Between 1965 and 1997 the National Endowment of the Arts expanded roughly tenfold. A good deal of this expansion involved local opera, dance, and theater companies, which does not, however, merely mean spreading arts projects out into the country from the once dominating urban centers; it also means spreading the ethos of the arts world into places that once might not have been so engaged by it. It is a well-known proposition that what the government pays for the country gets more and more of. In 1970 there were 720,000 people who identified themselves as "artists"; by 1998 there were 1,671,000. Nor is this the whole picture: by 1998 again, some 1.3 million Americans were working somewhere in the "nonprofit arts" sector—spreading the new taste to the heretofore unenlightened far and wide. Need it be said that the crucifix in urine and displays of the photography described above received government support—as did the show that featured the so famously besmirched painting of the Virgin?

The *Washington Times*, throughout its history, seemed to be in the forefront of breaking story after story about scandalous, crude, and invidious artworks that had been supported by the federal government. This contributed in no small measure to the national uproar over what many in the country saw as taxpayer-supported sewage masquerading as genuine aesthetic works. The original avant-garde had once prided itself on, and taken a kind of strength from, the idea that it was outraging the great middle class, or bourgeoisie; but now, it seemed, there was no avant-garde "avant" enough to bring about much significant outrage.

And what held true for the arts also came to apply to the general enterprise of criticism, by which is meant the practice of introducing, explicating, and offering judgment on whatever lays claim to seriousness in the arts. This enterprise distributes its wares largely through the media of higher education and fashionable journalism. If the greater part of the public in the nineties (and after) continued to consume popular works that amused or otherwise immediately pleased them, the critical community nevertheless continued to make its influence felt: especially among those whose educational attainments and con-comitant social and economic outlook seemed to require a "higher" cultural outlook to match. Thus new literary and intel-lectual works of indifferent to negative achievement—not to mention those whose major if not only purpose, like the works of graphic "art" mentioned above, was to shock and offend the deepest sexual and religious sensibilities of a continuingly large sector of the public—continued to be touted and were fre-quently also highly profitable, for creator, distributor, and last, but not necessarily least, critical sponsor.

As for the offended public, it was by and large no simple matter for its feelings to find a truly satisfactory outlet. Offensive books could of course be left, unbought, on the shelves; offensive

plays and movies could be—and often were—left seriously unat-
tended. What could not be ignored, however, was the titillating or
disturbing or just plain cheap and vulgar fare offered to one's
children as necessary to their education, particularly in the higher
grades. Down through the years many thoughtful people had
become outright advocates of censorship, despite the bad name
censorship had long ago earned by the inability of its practi-
tioners to make the necessary distinctions between distinguished
and merely obscene works. By the nineties, however, the problem
of offensiveness had moved far beyond published works, and
even staged and filmed entertainment, and was now to be found
in such blatant public manifestations as clothing advertisements
in which the sexuality of beautiful young men and/or girls was
made unignorably explicit and obscene, and hateful recorded
popular music. The recording industry, devoted to hardening the
sensibilities of the young, did meet some public resistance: Tipper
Gore, for instance, had begun a campaign against the offending
lyrics, or at least their so easily accessible display, and some years
later William Bennett headed a committee of well-known public
figures who bearded the chief managers of one of the chiefly
offending corporations, the Time Warner Company, in their den
and demanded to know why so major an American industry
would be so negligent of the minds and spirits of the country's
young. Reading aloud to those present an example of a rap song
for whose widespread distribution Time Warner was responsible,
Bennett turned to the company's now somewhat disquieted CEO,
and demanded to know, " What kind of people are you?"

The answer, of course, is that they were people, as the old American saw has it, crying all the way to the bank. But notice of some kind had been served, notice, moreover, from a source not so easily dismissed as merely "kooky" or "extremist" religious fundamentalists—a designation with which all purveyors of the offending culture had for so long been comforting themselves. To be sure, no more than a warning shot had been fired across the bow. But readers of the public temper, which all for-profit purveyors of the popular culture must be, sooner or later, no matter how privately reluctant, could for their own benefit now perhaps begin to notice some shift in that temper. And on this front of the Culture War, the *Washington Times*, along with towering figures like Bennett, was a major player. Indeed, the paper devoted relentless coverage to the contretemps over sociopathic music lyrics, often breaking news exclusives that provided red meat for opponents of the new genre of decadence.

There were various signs of such a shift, from the once unimaginable success of William Bennett's *The Book of Virtues*, a collection of traditional stories and fables for children about the value of virtuous behavior, to the best-sellerdom of books written by authors as disparate as the historian Stephen Ambrose and the television anchor Tom Brokaw about the heroism as well as the deep brotherhood of the American soldiers who took part in World War II—works whose popularity represented a new resistance to the post-Vietnam ethos of the country's young.

New York City by itself provided a certain incontrovertible evidence of this shift, one example being the widespread popularity of New York mayor Rudy Giuliani, who with almost no resistance had, by cracking down on all petty forms of illegal or harassing behavior, as well as the banishment of sex shops to out-of-the-way neighborhoods, managed to make New York a safe and attractive enough city to be besieged with year-around hordes of tourists from everywhere. Other examples, from tell-tale to downright urgent, abound: in the growing assault, already mentioned, against the meager and literally valueless fare being offered the country's children by American public education; in the high profitability of such products as movies that appeal to children and their parents together, along with the spate of revivals of 1950s high-hearted musicals and the concomitant resistance to so much once acceptable "serious" theatrical fare; even, funnily enough, in the move within the high musical culture toward a new and fascinating combination of deep religious piety and tonality (perhaps "not yet ready," as they say, "for prime time," but promisingly given to beauty as that word was once understood by the human ear).

Politically, too, it was found advisable by a new Democratic president after 1992 to cover many of what had been his former left-leaning tracks and at the very least play the centrist. And last but not least, there was the continuing stirring of simple patriotism, begun in the election of Reagan but so largely overborne by the resistant noises of the old liberal culture, and yet still audible to those with ears willing to hear.

With few highly notable and honorable exceptions, among those generally unwilling to hear there was, and remains, the press. This term, the press, has, properly speaking, become a very wide one, including as it does not only the journals, daily, weekly, and monthly, but also the great, greedy maw of news and public affairs television. In the country's major cities, to be sure, newspapers have threatened to become a dying breed, overtaken as so many have been by the greater immediacy, reach, and profitability of television. Curiously, such once great liberal journalistic institutions as the *New York Times*, the *Washington Post*, and others seem not to understand how their piously and fashionably liberal advocacy with respect to the burning issues of education and culture could be eating into the production of their own future readerships: which appear from the evidence of the papers themselves to have grown smaller, more elite, and palpably less serious.

Moreover, among those elements of the press that are currently most successfully devoted to resisting the tide of unthinking piety that washes over so much of American journalism are a few newspapers and magazines published precisely for the sake of being a source of positive influence and moral suasion, the *Washington Times*, of course, being the prime example. And increasingly there came to be felt the enormous power of what used to be called narrowcasting, i.e., cable television, but can be called "narrow" no longer. For such channels as Fox News and MSNBC, both of them remarkably liberated from the traditional ethos of television news—and other local channels whose effect is difficult to measure but which have frequently offered local viewers a liberating array of choices—came during the nineties to undermine what had once been a virtually inescapable monopoly.

Alas, however, something other than either economics or late starting competition has been influential in the current shabby condition of so much of established American journalism. Indeed, it is the same thing that is responsible for a good deal, if not most, of the moral and intellectual disquiet described above. And like many another influence so unhappily manifested in the nineties, it had originally unfolded long ago and was the outgrowth of an unthinking desire to do good: that is, the massive, indeed near universal, expansion of something calling itself higher education.

This expansion began in the aftermath of World War II, as a means, through what was called the G. I. Bill, of providing both recompense and fresh opportunity to the millions of America's returning veterans. Under this bill, the government paid their tuition to a college largely of their choice, along with a small monthly stipend that would theoretically enable them to study full time and go on to a profession. To accommodate the veterans in turn required a massive expansion of existing colleges and universities and the creation of some new ones, naturally with a concomitant expansion of their faculties. During those early postwar years, then, the campuses had become unprecedentedly earnest places, full of students who were deeply serious about life and in a hurry to be getting on with it.

These veterans had at the same time set about fathering the famous postwar baby boom, which by the late 1960s would itself be setting off to swell the ranks of the college population—but with a difference: whereas higher education had been a way of compensating the veterans of World War II for the loss of time and, with it, livelihood, by the time the generation of their children came of college age, going on beyond high school would be considered not only a necessity but a kind of divine right. So it was that by the 1970s millions upon millions of kids had already entered, or would soon be entering, college.

Moreover, here, too, the civil rights movement had played a role: for something that had become key to its efforts at betterment of the lot of America's blacks was the idea that higher education would become the indispensable short and direct route out of the hopeless life of the ghetto and into the professional middle class. But in the course of this new and so well-intended development, three factors had been left out of account. One was that in the postwar years, under the sway of fashionably degraded theories of pedagogy, the country's public school systems had been turning out a large number of students plainly ill-prepared for serious intellectual training.

The second—for a long while the country's best-kept secret—was that in so swift and large an expansion as they had gone through, many of the colleges and universities themselves had inevitably been degraded. And the third factor was the additional pressure on these already pressed-upon institutions from the idea that they would now also be required to redress the society's injustices to blacks—that is, required to catch neglected black students up on what they had already failed to learn and beyond that to propel them ahead, if need be, by such means of arbitrary ascription as affirmative action and grade inflation. Ironically, then, so far from weakening the distinction between the members of the country's elite and its so-called common folk, the massification of higher education was serving if anything greatly to solidify it. For it had come to be commonly said—and if said often enough, believed—that without such an education, there would be practically no way one could earn one's bread except for low-level drudgery: the common elitist usage for such drudgery being "flipping burgers." Such an idea would prove fateful, not only for higher education itself—whose purpose had so largely been redefined as one to rescue everyone of whatever attainment for something that could be called a professional life—but for all those young men languishing on street corners and imbibing the idea that there was no self-respect to be had from the performance of workaday labor.

And it would also prove in a variety of ways to be culturally fateful. For instance, one of the more immediately visible effects was that on American journalism. For a large number of the country's journalists were now being university trained for their profession, and what followed from this is that they were to a very large extent becoming members in good standing of the American elite, with everything such standing has come to imply about cultural as well as political loyalties.

Whereas once newspapermen had enjoyed the reputation of harboring a deep-going suspicion of the words and works of government officials and public figures generally, as well as of taking special delight in exposing the dark truth behind various kinds of public pious display, now, as citizens of the society of "media," their own means of livelihood had become an untouchable piety in itself. Moreover, thanks to television and the easy crossing of lines among daily, periodical, and televised journalism, the best situated of them had become celebrities in their own right: peers, now, of the kind of celebrated figures it had once been their highest calling to expose. And for cynicism they had now substituted an almost churchly piety toward fellow members of the elite whose roles or beliefs or causes they had elected to befriend. The result has been an ever widening rift—widening, in the nineties, nearly to a point of no return—between the ordinary members of the public and those who are paid to keep them informed from day to day.

In general, a certain disregard for the nature and interests of one's country, of the kind mentioned earlier in connection with the celebration of Columbus's landing in the New World, seems to have become a besetting self-indulgence among the social and cultural elites in modern democratic societies. Perhaps this is the result of the difficulty in keeping for themselves many of the most visible marks of a once uniquely high status: money, fashionable dress, the signs of cultural attainment, etc. Or perhaps it is for some other reason. The point is that with the vast expansion of the number of Americans who were now laying claim to being members of the country's educated class came a new wave of people feeling the need to distinguish themselves from those who might appear to be crowding them. And the major universities, richer and much expanded and newly powerful, seemed happy to oblige. They, too, it seemed, were involved in a process of distinguishing themselves, in this case from their earlier condition of high academic gentility, and had moved into a new world of power and celebrity. Fashion after fashion swept the campus, fashions political, philosophical, and literary. And since many present members of the faculties were now those who had been students in the 1960s and 1970s and had famously taken part in the assault on their universities in the 1960s and 1970s for being elitist, stodgy, and "irrelevant," there was with only a few honorable exceptions among the institutions of alleged higher learning, no resistance to the way a great deal of meretricious theorizing was passing for education. (Not that there had been any very widespread resistance from these same institutions at the time of the original assault on them.)

Various streams were now feeding into what had become a kind of general national swamp: to begin with, studies devoted not to training black students to better their lot in life but rather to reveling in the history of their oppression; feminist studies devoted to keeping young women, no matter how bright their futures, unpleasant and resentful about their lot in life and ready to march; literary studies devoted to "deconstructing" the very idea of common meaning along with the possibility of exercising relative judgments of quality and importance; sociological and political studies devoted primarily to documenting a whole wide range of American malfeasances, past and present, historical,

political, and economic; in some places, religious studies
engaged in demonstrating the all-around flexibility and open-
endedness of religious belief; and in a growing number of places
"gay" studies, designed to stir the homosexual students to the
same kinds of resentful activism as women's studies had stirred
among the young women.

Naturally, the above did not entirely characterize the full
extent of the nineties academy. In many places there were highly
visible individual exceptions among the faculty, and there were
some few and notable exceptions among the institutions as well.
But on the whole there was no question that, almost exactly in
proportion to its having become more essential to the future
well-being of the young in the eyes of the American public,
American higher education had fallen into—no other word will
do—a parlous condition. And with the kind of irony that
seemed particularly to beset the nineties, the more parlous, the
more culturally overbearing. Right at the center of this whole
academic imbroglio, not surprisingly, was the *Washington Times*,
running a steady stream of articles about the strange happenings
of political correctness at campus after campus across the
country. The paper also devoted precious ink to individual professors and institutions, like the National Association of
Scholars, that were paddling furiously against the PC tide. None
of the cultural issues that would set an ever growing public's
teeth on edge during that final decade of the millennium, then,
could be accounted a new one (with the possible exception of a
determined campaign for the legitimation of homosexual mar-

riage). The gathering power of public disaffection—evidenced not only in the assault on public education and a more noisy hostility to the media, but on such phenomena as a variety of new movements to reclaim the importance of the traditional family, and especially fatherhood, along with increasingly significant research on the immiserating effects of divorce—felt to the growingly disaffected to be overmatched by an ever more latitudinarian, and ever self-confident, culture.

The election of 2000 would only serve to confirm this impression for those on both sides of this divide. For the country appeared to the naked eye to be exactly split, not just between Democratic and Republican voters but as the electoral map so vividly showed, between the centers of the liberal culture on both coasts and the great middle stretching between them. The moment of full-scale discovery that the country had in fact, even if unconsciously, been turning in a new direction and was no longer prepared to be so careless with its virtue or so heedless of its real needs would not arrive until a day in September of 2001. But that day, all unbeknownst to everyone but the most prescient, had in fact been prepared for in the years leading up to it. The academy, it seemed, would for the most part remain loyal to its bad old political and intellectual habits, as would a certain number of blindly liberal politicians and media personalities. But the flags were now flying from every rooftop and every street corner, and as the whole country seemed to be heaving a great unconscious sigh of relief, with them were flying all the old, no longer dusty, flags of honor, country, duty, and family. What would happen into the long future no one could be so brazen as to say, but one thing was certain: the generation of America's children who were now coming of age and those who would be coming of age in the second decade of the new millennium were now being well inoculated against the kind of disease that had once, against little resistance, carried off so many of their elders.

Washington's Conscience

ARNOLD BEICHMAN

Arnold Beichman

Arnold Beichman is a research fellow at the Hoover Institution in Stanford, California. A former journalist and political science professor, he writes a regular column for the *Washington Times* and has authored six books, including *CNN's Cold War Documentary: Issues and Controversy.*

essimism about the future of democracy was widespread in the 1980s. Whittaker Chambers had openly wondered whether if in deserting the Soviet cause in favor of democracy he had chosen the losing side. Jean-François Revel was deeply pessimistic about the democratic future. *How Democracies Perish*, published in 1984, was the title of one of his books. Few reviewers derided the distinguished French philosopher for his pessimism. There was a tongue-in-cheek book and even a spoof movie about what would happen in the unlikely case of a "friendly" Soviet takeover of America. Few believed such a takeover was possible—but supposing it did happen? The important fact about those years of pessimism is that there was one man who was not a pessimist. Our chief executive, Ronald Reagan, was our chief optimist—unlike his predecessor. Jimmy Carter's snap judgment that the American people were suffering from a "malaise" was surely a case of mistaken identity as to who was suffering from a "malaise." And it was during such a mood that the *Washington Times* was established.

Imagine if during the past twenty years Washington had been a one-newspaper town. The *Washington Star* had folded, and there was only one newspaper voice in the capital city of the most powerful nation in the world. In 1981, a new conservative administration had come to Washington. The Reagan administration was determined to revive an economy which had been run into the ground by high interest rates, 11 percent unemployment, and soaring inflation, and was equally determined to bring down peacefully the evil Soviet empire by a policy of ever increasing military strength.

The new boy in town, President Ronald Reagan, was a happy warrior. But he was not alone in Washington. Besides his congressional supporters and the voting public, the president could count on another "new boy" in town: the *Washington Times*, founded on May 17, 1982, by the Reverend Sun Myung Moon. From the very first day, the *Times* dared to speak in what Washington liberal elites regarded as a discordant voice.

For example, the *Washington Times*'s editorial page and news columns in November 1982 derided the cheerleaders for Leonid Brezhnev's successor, a hard-liner named Yuri V. Andropov, as head of the Soviet Union. Andropov was built up in the *New York Times* and *Washington Post* as a jolly chap who liked to drink scotch and read American novels; therefore, peace was on the way. His ferocious record as longtime chief of the KGB secret police was pooh-poohed. But such nonsense was not to be found in the *Washington Times*. Its editors and columnists knew *disinformatsiya* when they saw it. And when a Soviet fighter plane shot down a civilian Korean airliner, Flight 007, which had strayed over Sakhalin Island on September 1, 1983, killing 269 passengers and crew, the *Washington Times*'s assessment of Andropov was tragically confirmed.

Right from the word go, the *Washington Times* was uncompromisingly anti-Soviet and anticommunist. It repudiated the prevalent Washington mood so graphically described by Midge Decter: anti-anticommunism and anti–free markets, and pro-political correctness, pornography posing as art or letters, gay rights, moral equivalence, Marxism, and its concomitant offshoot, anti-Americanism. To this ideological mélange was added a perverted racism against whites inspired by a well-known intellectual, Susan Sontag:

> The white race is the cancer of human history. It is the white race and it alone—its ideologies and inventions—which eradicates autonomous civilizations wherever it spreads, which has upset the ecological balance of the planet, which now threatens the very existence of life itself. (*Partisan Review*, Winter 1967)

The power of the Left academy was to be seen in what has happened in the field of history. Professor Kenneth S. Lynn of Johns Hopkins University wrote that "self-criticism is now so rampant in American culture, that many historians simply cannot deal with the principal achievements of the American past unless they can think of ways to discredit them." Writing in the context of a just-published history book, Professor Lynn wrote that the author "would have us believe that the nation's most spectacular achievement of the first half of the nineteenth century, to wit, the extension of its principle of free democratic republicanism across the width of an entire continent, was first and foremost a victory for a racist ideology of quasi-Hitlerian viciousness."

But there was now a dissident voice in Washington journalism every day of the week. In establishing another voice, not an echo, the *Washington Times* had begun to do what needed to be done if American democracy was to be secure and robust. The *Washington Times* defined what it supported in an editorial published February 14, 1983: "A strong America, reliably dedicated to freedom everywhere, is the central idea of Reaganism." The Cold War has now been over for more than a decade, and forgotten is the struggle against Soviet imperialism waged by President Reagan and passionately supported by the *Washington Times* in its commentary and editorial pages.

By influencing U.S. foreign policy, the *Washington Times* had begun to influence the course of American history. Its daily presence in the halls of Congress, the White House, government offices, and public service organizations began to weigh in heavily on the side of conservatism and against the febrile liberalism that had marked the previous White House. Its editorials and columns began to show up in speeches and statements of influential political figures, many of whom in the past had been unable to circulate their views regularly and in detail.

A century and a half ago, Thomas Carlyle, the great nineteenth-century British historian, looked at the press gallery in the House of Commons. Recalling the words of Edmund Burke about the estates in Parliament (priesthood, aristocracy, and commons), Carlyle said:

> Burke said there were Three Estates in Parliament; but, in the Reporters' Gallery yonder, there sat a Fourth Estate more important than they all. It is not a figure of speech, or a witty saying; it is a literal fact.... Printing, which comes necessarily out of Writing, I say often, is equivalent to Democracy: invent Writing, Democracy is inevitable.... Whoever can speak, speaking now to the whole nation, becomes a power, a branch of government, with inalienable weight in law-making, in all acts of authority. It matters not what rank he has, what revenues or garnitures: the requisite thing is that he have a tongue which others will listen to; this and nothing more is requisite.

The *Washington Times* arrived in the nation's capital at a crucial moment in world history, at a time when the Soviet Union was, as Richard Pipes points out in his essay, at the peak of its global expansionist power—North Korea, Vietnam, Cambodia, Ethiopia, Cuba, Chile, Nicaragua, El Salvador, Afghanistan, and, of course, the Soviet East European satellites. The editors were mandated to cover and comment on events and opinions that were routinely overlooked in the daily battle of ideas. But above all, the *Washington Times*'s code was based on the necessity to cover the day's events as objectively as possible and to leave to the editorial and op-ed pages the essential interpretation of those events. The op-ed and commentary pages were opened to writers and intellectuals, scholars, journalists. Readers discovered a whole new world of ideas that had hitherto remained buried in academic precincts.

How well the *Washington Times* reflected the views of the American people and how estranged was the elite media from those views can be seen in a forgotten episode in American history, one which shook, if only temporarily, the jaunty self-esteem of the elite media. On October 25, 1983, the U.S. Navy invaded the Caribbean island of Grenada to prevent a Soviet takeover. One Cuba, in President Reagan's view, was enough. The U.S. land and sea invasion, strongly supported by the *Washington Times*, went off without a hitch and without a single representative of print or electronic media as witness. Particularly fascinating was that the American public, according to public opinion polls, was delighted that President Reagan had excluded the press from this historic event. Reporters were invited for a look-see after it was all over.

A hurricane of protest by the media blew up in the invasion aftermath. John Chancellor bumbled about the public's "right to

know." Five hundred letters and phone calls to NBC came in right after his broadcast: they were five to one in favor of the ban against media surveillance of the invasion. Peter Jennings was astonished to find that 99 percent of his viewer mail supported Reagan. (He was equally astonished when the Nicaraguan Sandinistas, whose victory at the polls he had passionately predicted, lost the presidential election in 1990.) *Time* magazine reported that mail in favor of the Grenada ban ran eight to one in favor of President Reagan's edict.

Max Frankel, then editorial page editor of the *New York Times*, wrote: "The most astounding thing about the situation was the quick, facile assumption by some of the public that the press wanted to get in, not to witness the invasion on behalf of the people but to sabotage it." Had a latter-day, pro-Stalin Walter Duranty or Harold Denny or pro-Castro Herbert L. Matthews (three noted *New York Times* foreign correspondents) been part of an invasion press pool, expectation of the sabotage option might well have been realistic. A similar brouhaha, described in Lee Edwards's essay, occurred during the Gulf War.

How could smart journalists become so insensible to the feelings of their readers? Dr. Stanley Rothman, director of the Study for Social and Political Change at Smith College and a longtime student of the American media, had an answer about the television networks which could well apply to the print media:

"They ignore these people because it would require a change in how they view the world. The majority of journalists strive to be fair, but they are not dead horses, so they tend to be left of center. And the public as a whole knows it. Plus, the journalism schools and those who teach in them are more to the left than the journalists themselves."

————

The history-making role of the *Washington Times* came on the heels of three epoch-making episodes, as enumerated in Paul Johnson's essay: the election of Pope John Paul II in 1978, the victory of Margaret Thatcher in Great Britain in 1979, and the election of Ronald Reagan in 1980. What an extraordinary convergence of events! As Johnson argues: "[H]istory is made primarily by the willpower of great human personalities rather than by anonymous forces." Who could have believed that this triumvirate, each of them in a unique way, would without bloodshed or battle help bring about the downfall of Soviet totalitarianism, the unification of Germany, and the liberation of Eastern Europe and the Baltic states?

The *Washington Times* was the first newspaper to call for recognition of this signal event, the fall of the Soviet Union, by asking the president to designate November 9, the night the Berlin Wall came down in 1989, as World Freedom Day. Standing before the Berlin Wall two years earlier, President Reagan had apostrophized:

"General Secretary Gorbachev, if you seek peace, if you seek prosperity for the Soviet Union and Eastern Europe, if you seek liberalization: Come here to this gate. Mr. Gorbachev, open this gate. Mr. Gorbachev, tear down this wall."

I wrote in my *Washington Times* column November 9, 1991:

On November 9, 1989, a hated symbol of 70 years of communist tyranny came to a squalid end. The fear of nuclear war between the two superpowers was over. World peace seemed more assured than ever before in modern history.

November 9 from this day forward should be a day for world observance. In years to come we will realize that the man whose policies made that victory possible was Ronald Reagan.

Let us remember that this victory came without bloodshed, without marching armies, without loss of life, without nuclear fallout. Unprecedented in modern times, victor and vanquished together have acclaimed the end of the Cold War. Everybody won. November 9 each year would be a warning to future tyrants that tyranny, whether military as in Burma or ideological as in China and Cuba, has no future.

November 9, World Freedom Day.

The idea remained unrealized before being resurrected by President George W. Bush this year. On November 9, 2001, he issued a proclamation declaring the day which marked the anniversary of the fall of the Berlin Wall "World Freedom Day."

"Since the fall of the Berlin Wall, many countries have achieved freedom via the ballot box, through political pressure rising from their citizens, or as a result of the settlement of internal or regional conflicts," Mr. Bush said. "We celebrate the new freedom in which much of the world lives today."

Regarding my column, I would like to take this opportunity to answer a question about the *Washington Times* that has persisted for several years: Does the Unification Church dominate the *Washington Times*'s editorial content? I can speak for myself. In twenty years of writing for the *Washington Times* I have never been censored or had a column rejected. I am sure the same is true of my colleagues. I can remember when I first began my association with the paper that several friends and acquaintances here in Washington and in New York advised me strongly not to join the *Washington Times*'s writing community, that to do so would only injure my career. As, first, a visiting scholar fresh from the academy as a political scientist and, later, as a research fellow at the Hoover Institution, I have survived the dire warnings. In fact, a number of those who warned me two decades ago against writing for the *Washington Times* have more recently on occasion sought my advice, gladly given, on how their views could find an outlet in the *Washington Times* opinion pages.

Of course, there was a harmony of views between *Washington Times* writers and editors, but there were also disagreements. The onetime editor of the paper, Arnaud de Borchgrave, took a more optimistic view of President Mikhail Gorbachev's perestroika and glasnost policies than I did. My view was not at all optimistic but our differences had no effect on my writings in the *Washington Times*.

———

At present, the campaign against the *Washington Times* has quieted down. Looking back at the *Times*'s coverage of the eight Reagan years and the eight Clinton years, one can see that the paper had reached into opinion-making parts of Washington which welcomed discordance of views.

But there was another area in which the *Washington Times* made an important contribution to the battle of ideas and to the health of public debate. It provided an arena for defenders of tradition, family, faith, race-free decision making, and, as Lee Edwards puts it in his essay, "building on America's Judeo-Christian heritage." Quite true, there were other arenas—*National Review*, *Commentary*, the *American Spectator*, *Human Events*, the *Weekly Standard*—whose contributions to this battle of ideas were enormous, essential, and influential. However, through its editorials, columns, and news coverage the *Washington Times* provided a daily report and did it in the capital city of the most powerful country in the world, a strategic location for any publication.

In the important cultural-news arena, the *Washington Times* gave thorough coverage to both sides of the issues, especially on

topics shunned by left-leaning news organizations, such as abortion, sexual abstinence, the Promise Keepers evangelical Christian men's movement, and homosexuals in the military.

On abortion, the *Times* has always given the annual March for Life prominent coverage, not because the paper tilts pro-life but because the event is genuinely worthy of media focus. Every year, the march attracts many tens of thousands of people to the streets of Washington, D.C., and is often addressed (especially during Republican administrations) by the president himself.

When the issue of partial-birth abortion rose around 1993 and began getting into the news, the *Times* gave big coverage to the story—noting over and over physicians' testimony that the procedure is virtually never advised to protect the life of the mother. At first, other major media ignored it, but partial-birth abortion soon became a leading issue in a wide array of elections on the local, state, and federal levels.

Concerning sexual abstinence, the *Times*, unlike its liberal cousins in the print and broadcast media fields, has given space to many proponents of abstinence-only sex education in the public schools. Most important, perhaps, are the many opinion columns the paper has run, by a host of commentators whose views would otherwise probably not have been heard outside of a small circle of readers or listeners.

Typical of these columns is one by Cal Thomas, who wrote in a June 2001 essay: "I do not believe in a doctrine of inevitability when it comes to teens and sex. The Best Friends [abstinence education] approach works. You can see success in members' eyes. You can see what purity it has brought to their lives. Why aren't more people embracing such programs? It is because the sex industry makes money off young minds and bodies. The industry would go broke if abstinence among youth were to become a trend."

On coverage of the Promise Keepers, the men's movement started by former college football coach Bill McCartney, the *Washington Times* opinion pieces have been almost universally laudatory of the group, while those on the other side of the divide have been far more often critical or derisive than positive.

A sampling of news headlines is also revealing. In the *Washington Times*, there appeared the following: "Promise Keepers Leery of Politics; Members Want Focus on God, Family" (October 6, 1997); "Women Join Promise Keepers to Express Their Own Gratitude" (October 5, 1997); "Promise Keepers Pack the Mall; Men Asked to Give All Back Home" (October 5, 1997); "Men's Ministry Adds Thrill of Sports to Work of God" (May 26, 1995).

In the *Washington Post* were the following: "He's the Coach for the Faithful—Or the Far Right?" (September 28, 1997); "Promise Keepers' Success Also Measured in Dollars; Group Has Rapidly Become a Big Business" (September 29, 1997); "Voices of Protest Raised on the Mall; Feminists and Atheists Are Suspicious of Prayer Rally's Agenda" (October 5, 1997); and "Promise Keepers—And Doubters; Not All Clerics Are Rallying Behind Men's Religious Group" (September 13, 1997).

As to allowing homosexuals to serve openly in the military, a signature campaign promise of President Bill Clinton, the *Times* reported even before Clinton's inauguration that the new administration was facing overwhelming resistance in the ranks. Senior Pentagon correspondent Rowan Scarborough wrote that "enlisted personnel, junior officers, and four-star generals are expressing deep-seated opposition to allowing openly homosexual men and women to serve in one of the nation's most tradition-bound institutions."

He also reported that Clinton's policy was dead on arrival even among key congressional Democratic leaders like Senator Sam Nunn, chairman of the Senate Armed Services Committee, and Defense Secretary-designate Les Aspin.

The *Times* ran story after story on every aspect of the issue, while the *New York Times*, the *Washington Post*, and other media favoring the Clinton policy ran sympathetic page one articles on the general theme that gay soldiers were just like everyone else in the military.

The television networks and major newspapers also ignored or belittled stories about blacks in the armed services who were outraged at the effort to exploit civil rights to gain homosexuals access to the military. For example, the *Times*'s editors ran a page one story about Lt. Gen. Calvin Waller, the Army's second-in-command of Operation Desert Storm, who said to the Senate Armed Services Committee that he found it "offensive" that homosexuals were trying to equate their struggle for special rights with the fight against racism that blacks had waged for decades. He testified that the Clinton plan to allow open homosexuals to serve in the military would make it a "second-rate force."

The importance of the *Washington Times*'s presence in the nation's capital is that it supplied another way of looking at the day's events. Its editors and writers helped create a real debate on fundamental issues—political, intellectual, moral, and cultural—and afforded participants a channel by which their analyses and, if you will, prejudices, could be disseminated. Washington is no longer, journalistically speaking, a "one opinion" town. And in a democracy a clamor of opinions is a remedy for a nation's ills. There was no daily voice for conservatism in Washington, D.C., at a time when one-third of the American public defined itself as conservative while only 17 percent defined itself as liberal. And by conservatism, I mean a belief in a functioning capitalist economy and a constant insistence on the laws of the market, a strengthening of civil society, resistance to the "adversary culture," elevating the family as the crucial unit of a free society, and a disbelief in the "redeeming" power of institutions to transform reality.

Above all, the *Washington Times* was unabashedly anticommunist and anti-Soviet. What that meant was well expressed by Diana Trilling, a leading American intellectual, who in a mordant essay on J. Robert Oppenheimer wrote that "a staunch anticommunism was the great moral-political imperative of our epoch." What the pages of the *Washington Times* opposed was what Vaclav Havel, today president of the Czech Republic, called "the culture of the lie." The *Washington Times* sided with the defectors, dissidents, refuseniks, exiles, escapees like Milovan Djilas, Andrei Sakharov, Vladimir Bukovsky, Natan Sharansky, and so many others.

And here we come to a strange paradox which has concerned the *Washington Times* since the dissolution of the Soviet empire a decade ago. The global rebellion against command economies, the garrison state, socialism, and central planning is ignored by those public intellectuals who claim to be speaking for the masses. Utterly ignored are the lapidary words of Hilaire Belloc: "The control of the production of wealth is the control of human life itself." What that meant in statistical terms was the destruction by communist dictatorships of between eighty-five and 100 million human beings in the name of scientific socialism.

In a recent book, Professor Chalmers Johnson condemned the United States for seeking to "impose" a market economy on Asian countries. But that is precisely what the Asian urban masses have wanted: visit Hong Kong, Chinese coastal cities, and Taiwan, and study why people are willing to hurdle high voltage fences, to sail in leaky tubs in the South China Sea and across the Pacific, to risk asphyxiation in crowded freight cars, to fly in homemade planes—anything to get to the free market democracies. Professor Johnson, a *Washington Times* reviewer wrote, has failed to deal with the unofficial global plebiscite underway for decades against Marxist socialism and Marxism-Leninism by an almost unanimous vote among hundreds and hundreds of millions of people, victimized for generations by these baneful doctrines.

But Professor Chalmers Johnson is only one of many members of the academic profession who have utterly ignored the events of the last decade or, even worse, regret the fall of the Soviet empire and the popular repudiation of central planning and one-party dictatorships by its victims. They forget that some 10,000 missile launchers, most of them with multiple warheads, were targeted at the United States during President Reagan's years in office. But academics didn't forget to denounce him when he described the Soviet Union as "an evil empire."

Books have been written by historians, some of them distinguished like George F. Kennan, which deny there ever was a democratic victory in the Cold War. To such historians, one could apply the verdict of Richard Bernstein, the *New York Times* literary critic: "For many historians, history has become advocacy." George Kennan wrote in his memoirs: "Nobody 'won' the Cold War."

Yet in 1969 he wrote: "The retraction of Soviet power from its present bloated and unhealthy limits is essential to the stability of world relationships."

Just thirty years later, there is no Soviet power, its "bloated and unhealthy limits" having been totally retracted. There isn't even a Soviet Union. Did not, then, the democracies win the Cold War? Didn't the once Soviet-satellized countries of Central Europe and the Baltic "win" the Cold War? When the Berlin Wall came down followed by German reunification, wasn't that victory? Apparently not for Mr. Kennan and others of his ilk who never tell us how they define victory.

Or for Professor Ronald Steel, who offered this grudging verdict on freedom's bloodless victory over Soviet totalitarianism: "We have won a victory, of sorts."

Would Professor Steel describe our triumph over Nazism as "a victory, of sorts"? Perhaps we won the Cold War, he writes, "yet this is an ambiguous victory." But the ambiguity Steel ascribes to the situation is difficult to perceive. The onetime "evil empire," as President Reagan called it to contemptuous jeers from the liberal-left, is no more; democracy is alive where once dictators reigned.

Professor Steel, like others of his liberal persuasion, seems to regret the end of the Cold War. He writes: "In its perverted way, the Cold War was a force for stability."

Indeed, if by "stability" one means uprisings in East Germany and Hungary, Poland, Czechoslovakia, the trampling of human rights, the war in Afghanistan, Soviet support for the Yom Kippur war of aggression against Israel, the ubiquity of the KGB, and the Cuban missile crisis.

On the other hand, Steel writes that the Cold War was, "dangerous, wasteful, obsessive, and at times irrational." Stated in other words, unstable.

More than a decade ago, City University of New York professor John P. Higgins wrote that the field of American history "has come to be dominated by Marxists and feminists." And, he added, "the New Left is an idea whose time has passed and whose power has come." Professor Gertrude Himmelfarb has written that "Marxism has succeeded . . . in demeaning and denigrating political events, institutions, activities and ideas."

Responsible for this corruption in the study and teaching of history are not only Marxists, but another cadre of historians who helped create the era of political correctness: mainstream historians of high repute who seem to have been discombobulated by the sudden end of the Cold War during the two-term presidency of Ronald Reagan. Following from these and other examples of mainstream historical writing came the verdict of the late historian Wilcomb E. Washburn that "not even the shock of the collapse of Communist theory and power has been sufficient to cause the officers of one of the principal organizations of American historians—who present the institutional face of American history to the public at home and abroad—to express regret for their failure to speak up for truth in the past."

Washburn was talking about the American Historical Association (AHA) where, Professor Thomas C. Reeves has written,
"leftist ideology had dominated the historical profession for
some three decades. Race, class and gender, by this time, had virtually excluded all other topics of discussion in journals and at
historical meetings, while diplomatic, intellectual, political and
economic studies were barely tolerated."

The result of such pedagogy was to be found in an Associated
Press report which disclosed that nearly 80 percent of seniors at
fifty-five top colleges and universities, including Harvard and
Princeton, received a D or an F on a thirty-four-question high
school-level test on American history. While there was some difficulty in identifying James Madison as the principal architect of
the Constitution they all knew that "Beavis and Butthead" were
TV cartoon characters.

Despite this discomforting evidence, the post-Twin Towers
catastrophe produced the demand to study Islam more closely,
which to quote Dr. Lynne V. Cheney, "implies that it was our
failure to understand Islam that led to so many deaths and so
much destruction . . . If there were one aspect of schooling from
kindergarten through college to which I would give added
emphasis today, it would be American history."

———————

What of the future of the *Washington Times* in a country that has
undergone an unprecedented disaster? Since September 11, 2001,
the United States has confronted an enemy who accomplished

what was regarded as impossible. For eight years, from 1993 to 2001, it is now admitted (and so reported in the *Washington Times*), little was done in the highest seats of power to prepare for what, belatedly, seems to have been inevitable.

Pearl Harbor was a day in infamy which brought the U.S. into World War II. But there was another, later, wakeup call which shook America out of its lethargy. It was October 4, 1957, when the Soviet Union launched Sputnik I, the world's first artificial satellite. It was about the size of a basketball, weighed only 183 pounds, and took about ninety-eight minutes to orbit the Earth on its elliptical path. That launch ushered in new political, military, technological, and scientific developments.

While the Sputnik launch was a single event, it marked the start of the space age and the U.S.–USSR space race. A month later the Soviets launched Sputnik II with a heavier payload, including a dog named Laika. And the country, under the leadership of President Eisenhower and American science and industry, went to work.

The Sputnik launch also led directly in July 1958 to congressional passage of the Space Act and the creation of the National Aeronautics and Space Administration (NASA). And then, with a restoration of America's self-confidence, began our country's unduplicated space achievements with more to come.

Such a dynamic demonstration of recovery by an aroused and reenergized America is now history. Today's crisis is of a different order of magnitude and its character was perhaps best summarized more than a century ago by Otto von Bismarck,

Prussia's "Iron Chancellor," who said: "We live in a wondrous time in which the strong is weak because of his moral scruples and the weak grows strong because of his audacity."

For the *Washington Times*, its editors, and everyone else, the radical Islamist challenge is one that will involve America and other democracies in new and even more dangerous confrontations. Meeting that challenge will demand a unity of purpose and leadership and audacity of the strong, invigorated by a will to safeguard and extend democratic freedoms. But that struggle against the radical Islamist challenge will face a challenge at home: the defection from the democratic resistance by fellow Americans with intellectual credentials like Susan Sontag, Norman Mailer, Eric Foner, and Noam Chomsky, who have exonerated the terrorists and who blame America for September 11. Ms. Sontag, an admirer of Castro and Ho Chi Minh, in a post-September 11 commentary in the *New Yorker* magazine, placed the guilt for the tragedy on the United States, or, to quote her words in the *New Yorker*, "an attack on the world's self-proclaimed superpower, undertaken as a consequence of specific American alliances and actions."

Ms. Sontag was not alone in her malevolent alienation. There were others. A sampling collected by the American Council of Trustees and Alumni (ACTA) came up with these choice items:

Professor Peter Zedrin of Brown University: "I was cheering when the Pentagon got hit because I know about the brutality of the military."

Professor William Keach also of Brown University: "What happened on September 11 was terrorism, but what happened during the Gulf War was also terrorism."

Professor Richard Berthold of the University of New Mexico: "Anyone who can blow up the Pentagon gets my vote."

Professor Barbara Foley of Rutgers University: "[W]e should be aware that, whatever its proximate cause, its ultimate cause is the fascism of U.S. foreign policy over the past many decades."

And, perhaps, the most repellent post-September 11 statement was that by Barbara Kingsolver, a feminist, about how the American flag "stands for intimidation, censorship, violence, bigotry, sexism, homophobia, and shoving the Constitution through a paper shredder."

To use Disraeli's metaphor in another context, the United States is today two nations, comprising the vast majority of the American people and a powerful, disaffected intellectual class, young and old, whose anti-Americanism dominates the American academy. According to a poll reported by ACTA, 92 percent of American voters answered "yes" when asked whether Americans should take action against the attack of September 11, even if it meant thousands of casualties. The same question posed to Harvard students elicited a 28 percent favorable response rate. Columnists such as Thomas Sowell, Cal Thomas, Suzanne Fields, Jonah Goldberg, Mona Charen, Walter Williams, Linda Chavez, and others have responded in the pages of the *Washington Times* to this academic defection from democracy and defamation of America and provided some balance in the debate.

Recently in his book *The Reckless Mind: Intellectuals in Politics*, University of Chicago professor Mark Lilla posed this question: "What is it about the human mind that made the intellectual defense of tyranny possible in the 20th century?" It is one of the anomalies of our time that highly intelligent people willingly and actively supported Lenin, Stalin, Hitler, or Mao during the twentieth-century supremacy of these master genocidists. These irrationalist intellectuals—a "chorus for tyranny," Professor Lilla calls them—all lived in democratic societies. Therefore, their assent was born not out of fear, but out of a conscious decision to ignore reason. Professor Lilla has coined a phrase for these reckless minds: the "philotyrannical intellectual." This "social type," he says, comprised "distinguished professors, gifted poets, and influential journalists [who] summoned their talents to convince all who would listen that modern tyrants were liberators."

In his recently published study, "Public Intellectuals: A Study of Decline," Richard Posner (a public intellectual as well as a U.S. Court of Appeals judge) ascribes to this group a "proclivity for taking extreme positions, a taste for universals and abstractions, a desire for moral purity, a lack of worldliness, and intellectual arrogance." These attributes, he writes, "work together to induce in many academic public intellectuals, selective empathy, a selective sense of justice, an insensitivity to context, a lack of perspective, a denigration of predecessors as lacking moral insight, an impatience with prudence and sobriety, a lack of realism and excessive self-confidence."

The striking consequence about these failures to serve truth is the academic intellectual's malignant influence on society. For as Lionel Trilling, the great critic of the "adversary culture," a phrase he coined, once wrote: "This is the great vice of academicism, that it is concerned with ideas rather than with thinking and nowadays the errors of academicism do not stay in the academy; they make their way into the world and what begins as a failure of perception among intellectual specialists finds its fulfillment in policy and action."

Just as a powerful class of intellectuals influenced the course and inglorious end of the war in Vietnam a quarter century ago, so these same intellectuals and their acolytes, Norman Podhoretz has predicted, will—if not resisted—hinder the military mobilization essential to resist radical Islamism. And resisting these members of the twenty-first-century New Left will be a continuation of the fight which the *Washington Times* undertook twenty years ago in the nation's capital where once there was only one daily newspaper voice.

When the true history of contemporary America is written one day, those whose bylines have graced the news and editorial pages of the *Washington Times* will see how a newspaper, produced by journalists and co-opted public intellectuals and academics, became what President George W. Bush told the editor of the *Washington Times*: "You're a conscience of this town."

Index

1990s: abortion and, 130–34; arts
and, 154–56; assisted suicide
and, 135–36; blacks and,
136–42; capitalism in, 22–23;
education and, 143–48,
165–66; as end of history, 20;
gay rights and, 151–54; human
gene research and, 134–35;
media and, 160–64; offensiveness and, 157–60; welfare
reform and, 148–49; women
and, 149–51

ABC News, 45
abortion: 1990s and, 130–34;
Constitution and, 133; Culture
War and, x, xi; politics and,
130–34; Supreme Court and,
132–33; *Washington Times*
and, 182–83
Acquired Immune Deficiency
Syndrome (AIDS), 151
ACTA. *See* American Council of
Trustees and Alumni
Adams, John, 45
affirmative action, x, 137–38

Afghanistan, 33, 79–80, 111, 176;
bin Laden and, 35; commu-
nism and, 9; Soviet Union and,
7–8, 12; Taliban regime in, 34;
terrorism and, 53
Africa, 5
AHA. *See* American Historical
Association
A History of the American People
(Johnson), 2
AIDS. *See* Acquired Immune
Deficiency Syndrome
Allen, Henry, 78
Allen, Woody, 59
Alsthom-Atlantique, 116
Amanpour, Christiane, 52
Ambrose, Stephen, 158
American Council of Trustees
and Alumni (ACTA), 192
American Historical Association
(AHA), 190
American Spectator, 182
Andropov, Yuri, 11, 99, 108, 172
Angola, 9
Annenberg School of Communi-
cations, 49

anti-Americanism, 172–74,
    192–93
AOL Time Warner, 53
Apple, R. W., Jr., 80
Arabs, 32–33
Archibald, George, 65
Argentines, 17–18
Aristotle, 99–100, 119
Arkansas, 26
arts, 1990s and, 154–56
Asia: capitalism in, 21–24; Soviet
    Union and, 5
Asian Tigers, 22
Aspin, Les, 185
assisted suicide, 1990s and,
    135–36
Ataturk, 32

Baghdad, 20, 52
Balkanization, 15, 16
Balkans, 16
Baltic States, 15, 104
barbarism, 4
Barnes, Fred, 63, 79
Battle of Britain, 73, 78
BBC. *See* British Broadcasting
    Corporation
Begin, Menachem, 29
Beichman, Arnold, xi, xii, 170
Beijing, 13, 68
Beirut, 30
Belarus, 106

Belloc, Hillaire, 186
Bennett, William, 157, 158
Berlin Wall, ix
Bernstein, Carl, 43, 64
Berthold, Richard, 193
bilingual education, 142–43
bin Laden, Osama, ix, 34, 35
Bismarck, Otto von, 191–92
Blackmun, Harry, 133
Black Power, 149
blacks: 1990s and, 136–42; media
    and, 162–63
Black Sea, 9
black studies, 138–39
Blair, Tony, 4
Bobbit, Lorena, 59
Bolsheviks, 98
The Book of Virtues (Bennett),
    158
Bosnia, 16
Boxer Rebellion, 36
Bozell, L. Brent, 67
Brazelton, T. Berry, 70
Brezhnev, Leonid, 11, 172
Brezhnev Doctrine, 5
Britain: globalization and, 38;
    GNP of, 24; terrorism and, 31;
    Thatcher and, 6; U. S. relation-
    ship with, 18; Yugoslavia and,
    16
British Broadcasting Corpora-
    tion (BBC), 73